Geoff Elliott

For Trudi and Charlie

Special thanks to

Steve Littlejohns, Colin Grimshaw, Robert Davison and Atisa Mulji for their many corrections and helpful suggestions.

Alan Davidson for his valued guidance.

C. A. Elliott, FLA, for reading each draft and preparing the index.

This book accompanies the BBC Television series
Video Active first broadcast on BBC 1 from March 1987
The series was produced by Robert Albury

Published to accompany a series of programmes
prepared in consultation with the BBC Continuing
Education Advisory Council

© Geoff Elliott 1987
First Published 1987
Published by BBC Books
a division of BBC Enterprises Ltd,
35 Marylebone High St, London W1M 4AA

Typeset by Phoenix Photosetting, Chatham
Printed and bound in England by
Mackays of Chatham Ltd

This book is set in 10/11 Ehrhardt Linotron

ISBN 0 563 21314 0

Contents

Introduction

Camcorders, video cameras and videocassette recorders (VCRs) have never been so popular as they are now. Portable video is no longer a consumer luxury item. It has become a popular way of getting more enjoyment from family occasions, holidays, sports and hobbies. It is widely used in business and industry. Above all, making a video with sound is itself exciting and rewarding.

Whether you have your own equipment already, or are wondering what to get, this book will help you. It tells in a non-technical way how to make videos, and what accessories to buy. It shows, in everyday language, with clear diagrams, how to make videos that other people will enjoy watching. There are also dozens of ideas for video programmes and projects.

The book is set out in two parts. Part One has lots of useful information, hints and advice on getting started in video. Part Two is for those who want to get more involved and more ambitious. Each part is divided into sections covering equipment, techniques and applications. The sections are self-contained so that you can quickly refer to them whenever you need help. Use the index if you want to find all the information on a particular topic.

I hope that *Video Active* and the BBC TV series it accompanies will help you get more fun and enjoyment out of video.

Geoff Elliott
March 1987

PART ONE

Getting Started

Choosing and Using a Camcorder and Video System

Making movies with video is now more popular than ever. The dawn of the camcorder has started to catch our imagination. A camcorder is a combined video camera and videocassette recorder (VCR). It is specially designed for shooting video anywhere. There are many different types. All are small, lightweight, portable, battery-operated and easy to use. The smallest weighs only a couple of pounds, and is no larger than a paperback book. To rival them, separate systems of cameras and VCRs are getting smaller and lighter. And both camcorders and separate systems have higher quality pictures and sound than ever before.

The smallest camcorders are record-only machines. If you buy a record-only camcorder, you also have to buy a home-based machine which is the same format as the camcorder, in order to play back your tapes.

A record-only camcorder – the smallest of all VCRs.

The record-only camcorder is smaller and lighter than one which can play back as well—and quite a lot cheaper. So one of these might well suit you to add to an existing VCR. On the other hand, a record/playback model will allow you to playback direct to any TV via the aerial socket, as you would with a separate portable or mains-only VCR.

WHAT TO LOOK FOR IN A CAMCORDER

When choosing a camcorder you must, above all, look at picture and sound quality. If you decide on a record-only camcorder, check that it has all the features you need. For example, some models do not have an electronic viewfinder or a zoom lens, which might be limiting for the uses you have in mind. Because they are so light and compact, though, these 'go-anywhere' machines do recommend themselves for holidays, visits, and in the commercial world for site surveys and project management.

All the three small formats offer camcorders as part of their range, and the record/playback models are proving very popular. Smallest in size are the VHS–C and 8mm format camcorders. The versions which have a microchip imager instead of a conventional camera tube are particularly compact. But even the largest of the camcorders, which use tube electronics and the larger VHS and Betamax tapes are more transportable than separate systems.

These camcorders can form the basis of a complete video system. Some of them have a tuner-timer as an accessory with which you can record broadcast TV programmes (off-air recording) when it is attached to the camcorder.

There is intense competition between the manufacturers for the best picture and sound quality. VHS is now available with improved HQ (high quality) circuitry and hi-fi sound, whilst 8mm offers an additional sound-only mode on its top range VCRs, with digital audio comparable with compact disc players.

The camcorder is rapidly gaining many admirers in broadcast television. Betacam – a broadcast standard camcorder using Betamax tape running at faster than usual speed – is a particularly popular format for Electronic News Gathering (ENG).

A camcorder is compact and easy to use.

Camcorders were developed primarily for making videos. Although battery-operated, combined mains adaptors and battery chargers are available as accessories, allowing the camcorder to be run from the mains when needed.

COMPARING CAMCORDERS AND SEPARATE SYSTEMS

The most obvious difference between a camcorder and a camera/ VCR combination is that the camcorder has no connecting cable. The camera and VCR are combined in one unit. When a camera is used with a separate VCR the signal is fed into a special camera input on the VCR. Some VCRs do not have camera inputs. These can still be used with a separate camera. The camera cable is connected to a camera adaptor, and the video and audio signals are fed separately into the VCR, via Video In and Audio In sockets.

The pictures and sound are relayed to a TV from the camcorder or VCR RF Out socket to the aerial socket of the TV. Standard antenna (aerial) cable is used to make the connection. More sophisticated TVs, and all monitors, have Video and Audio In sockets, either separate, or a combined one (eg the AV Euroconnector, which can also carry computer RGB signals). These give a higher quality signal than RF. RF stands for radio frequency, a combined video and audio signal, which has to be modulated and then de-modulated from camcorder or VCR to TV, which accounts for the poorer quality pictures and sound.

A camera can be used with any VCR – but you may well have to use an adaptor to connect other makes of camera to your VCR. If you already have a VCR, and want to try out a camera, take it to a dealer who is prepared to take the time to connect a camera to it. You might be able to arrange a weekend hire before you commit yourself to rent or buy. Some dealers will deduct the cost of the hire from the purchase price.

Both portable and mains-only VCRs can be used with a camera. Adding a tuner-timer gives the portables the same facility for off-air recording as mains-only VCRs. If you want to use a camcorder for recording off-air TV programmes, you must check that you can get a compatible tuner-timer unit.

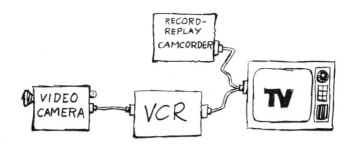

The record-replay camcorder connects directly to the TV.
The camera has an extra cable to the VCR.

Portable vcrs and camcorders are battery-operated – they draw their power from special rechargeable one piece batteries. As with camcorders, batteries for the portables are usually charged via the combined charger and mains units. Often the tuner-timer, mains adaptor and battery charger are one unit, although manufacturers now supply separate mains adaptor/chargers.

A portable separate system is flexible –
either the camera or the VCR can be upgraded.

In new condition, the internal battery usually lasts about 30 to 45 minutes when recording, before a charge is necessary. There are more powerful video batteries available as packs or belts which can be easily connected via adaptors to all portable video equipment. Although heavier and two to three times more expensive than the manufacturers' standard batteries, these battery packs and belts allow you to record freely for two hours or more before they need recharging. Adaptors are also available to run low voltage lighting off of these batteries.

When a video camera is connected to a separate vcr, it is also powered by the battery which fits inside the vcr. The power lead is in the multi-way cable which runs between camera and vcr. If you use a camera with a VCR of a different make, it is only possible to use battery power if the connectors on the camera and VCR are directly compatible, or if the camera is switchable between different makes of VCR. Otherwise, you will have to use a camera adaptor. It plugs directly into the mains, and to it you connect both the camera and VCR.

You can use a video camera with any mains-only VCR with a Video In socket, but you will need a camera adaptor.

Mains-only VCRs are fine for use with a camera. The main snag is that you will not be able to use it away from mains power. Also, the mains-only VCRs tend to be quite heavy, as they contain both the tuner-timer and recording components in one solid unit.

Playback only VCRs are available, but, of course, you can't record with these. These are mainly used by educational organisations and others who have a need to replay, but not necessarily record, videotapes.

When shooting video with camcorders and portable VCRs the majority give clean transitions between one shot and another when assembling a sequence or programme. On the other hand, mains-only VCRs generally suffer from annoying jitter (picture disturbance) between shots.

Some VHS mains-only VCRs are very difficult to cue up when

recording a series of shots, so that the next recording doesn't record over the ending of the previous recording. When trying one out with a camera, check that it will go direct from Play and Pause mode to Record and Pause. If the tape has to go to Stop in between the two modes (which involves the tape unloading and reloading round the head drum), accurate cueing up is almost impossible. This is a disadvantage of the slow tape speed of small-format domestic systems. The slightest difference in tape position will represent many frames of video, and almost certainly enough to lose the last few words or vital action of the previous shot. If you have no choice but to use such a machine, you will have to allow a longer than usual pause at the end of each shot to allow for this inaccuracy; this may well result in awkward pauses at the end of some shots, but that is better than losing picture or sound information.

Most portable VCRs have back-space editing which ensures clean edits between shots. To check it works, connect a camera and TV to the VCR, and record several different shots, starting and pausing the VCR using the camera trigger. Rewind and play back the shots. There should be clean edits between each. You will need to gauge the amount your VCR back-spaces in this way, as it will affect exactly where you stop recording a shot. If you stop recording too soon after someone has finished speaking, for example, you could lose the last word when the next back-space edit is recorded.

For continual recording, a record-review facility is useful, which will play back the last few seconds of a shot, and cue up just before the end, ready for the next shot. The edits between shots should once more be quite clean.

HOW TO CONNECT VIDEO TO A TV

The VCR or camcorder can be connected to the TV by antenna cable. To install a VCR for home viewing, disconnect the aerial lead from the TV aerial socket at the back of the TV (it simply pulls out of the socket), and plug it in to the socket on the back of the VCR which is marked 'Aerial' or 'RF In'. Now connect one end of a short antenna cable to the VCR socket marked 'RF Out' and the other end to the aerial socket of the TV.

Now the broadcast TV signal can feed from the aerial directly into the VCR and out again to the TV. So when recording off-air, it does not matter if the TV is on or off; it doesn't even have to be connected to the VCR. This is why you can watch one programme on the TV whilst recording another on the VCR.

If your TV has an AV Euroconnector or Audio and Video In sockets, then much better quality results will be gained by using them. Connection is either direct from an AV Euroconnector output socket on the VCR, or from the audio and video outputs, via an adaptor. Dealers can supply the appropriate cables.

WHAT MOST PEOPLE DO (ILLEGALLY) WITH THEIR VIDEO

In most homes, the VCR is used for recording broadcast TV programmes (off-air recording) for playing back at a different time. This use is often called time-shifting. Most TV programmes are subject to copyright. To record them without prior consent (which is rarely given) is thus illegal. A VCR can be programmed to record several programmes on different channels at different times. A VCR can also be used to record a programme on one channel whilst watching a programme on a second channel. Both these uses rely on the tuner-timer built into the VCR which is tuned to off-air broadcast channels in exactly the same way as a TV set.

A lot of people also rent tapes from a video library to play back on the video, which is certainly cheaper and often more convenient than going to the cinema. This is quite legal unless, of course, the tapes are pirate copies, or not licensed for rental or sale. Then it is illegal.

Copies can easily be made from one VCR to another. You can copy between any two formats, using a camcorder, portable, or mains-only VCR. Of course, record-only machines will only record, and playback-only ones will only play back. *Making copies of rented tapes and videograms, for home or commercial use, is illegal.*

You should have an instruction book for your VCR or camcorder. Read it carefully so that you understand all the controls and features available to you. You will find the main controls and features explained later in this section, but the location and exact operation of these will vary from one machine to another. If you don't have an instruction book, you can get one from the manufacturer.

HOW A VIDEO RECORDING IS MADE

Whether the video signal that enters the VCR or camcorder comes from a camera or from a tuner-timer it is electronically recorded onto videotape. When a recording is made, a video track and an audio track are recorded on tape at the same time. A control track is also recorded on the tape by the recording head. It has sync pulses (synchronised information) on it. When a blank tape is played back, the picture looks like snow; there is no control track, and therefore no recording.

The sync pulses provide a standard reference for the VCR when the tape is played back. Where there is a gap between recordings, there will be a break in the sync pulses. It is absence of sync pulses that causes pictures to 'heave' or jitter between separate recordings.

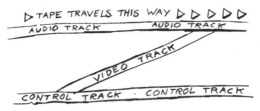

The invisible tracks which make up a video recording.

On Hi-Fi and stereo pre-recorded tapes, audio is recorded with the video track. These tapes also have a separate linear audio track, which is the one used for normal video sound recording with a camera. This linear track is sometimes divided in half, giving two audio tracks, but increasing tape noise.

WHAT VIDEOTAPE IS, AND HOW TO LOOK AFTER IT

Videotape is made up of a plastic base coated with a layer of metal particles which are magnetised in a varying pattern. The principle is similar to that used in audio tape recording. The number of different tracks on the tape varies from format to format, but since the extinction of the Philips 2000 system, all tape formats are single sided, ie they are not turned over like audio cassettes.

Videotape used to come on open spools like reel to reel audio tape. Nowadays, just as cassettes have become the popular norm for audio, so video cassettes have become the norm, except for certain broadcast applications. The tape is pre-wound onto spools and loads automatically into the VCR when you press the Record or Playback buttons. This means that handling the videotape is unnecessary, in fact, you should actively avoid touching the tape surface since the grease from your fingers can damage it.

Breaking a tape is now fairly uncommon. You can get repair kits which involve splicing the tape, but these should only be considered as a temporary measure until you can copy the tape. *Never* allow the spliced part of the tape to travel across the video heads. Any repairs have to be more bulky than the tape itself, and damage to the heads will certainly result.

Videotape may be stored for a long time before you buy it, which can cause the tape to settle and slacken. It is therefore important that all tapes are wound completely to the end and rewound before use. This is called a 'clean wind'.

Signals are recorded magnetically onto videotape by the VCR or camcorder. It is possible, therefore, for the tape to be re-magnetised or de-magnetised. This is what enables videotapes to be wiped and re-used. Beware, though, as in some situations you may accidently impair or lose your valuable recordings. The danger zone is anywhere near a magnetic field. So avoid placing tapes on loudspeakers, including TV sets, near transformers and electric motors. It has been known for tapes to be wiped by being taken on the London tube in a compartment over the motor! Heat and mechanical shock can also de-magnetise tapes.

Although videotape is very thin, it is quite strong and flexible, so it can stand up to many repeated recordings and playings. High Grade tapes are better than ordinary tapes because the quality control is better. The surface should stay intact for longer, so there should be fewer drop-outs. Drop-outs occur when areas of the tape surface lose the oxide, or metal particles, and appear on the TV screen as tiny white jittery speckles. Tapes are not that expensive, so when you can see drop-outs, throw the tape away.

You will, of course, want to keep tapes which have valued or irreplaceable recordings. In this case think about making a copy if the tape is going to be played a lot, so that the copy wears out rather than the original. You can always make further copies.

As with audio cassettes, videotapes have an erase protect tab which is removable when you have a recording which you want to keep. Removing the tab at the back of the cassette simply prevents the camcorder or VCR from entering Record mode. If you change your mind, it is a simple matter to tape over the hole with sticky tape known as masking tape, which will then allow you to record. Don't use sellotape for this as tapes become quite warm in use and when left in the VCR (which you shouldn't do), the tape will soon curl, and lose its adhesiveness. Damage might result if it finds its way inside the camcorder or VCR.

When you have finished with a tape, always rewind it before storing it away. If you don't, it will develop a kink at the point where it was left, which will show as interference on vision when the tape is played again.

Once you build up a stock of tapes, you may want to start an indexing and filing system. A blank book can be used as a simple index system, with separate sections for different types of programme. Label each tape with a number, date of recording and editing, and title. File the tapes and log them in your book, in numerical sequence, and keep the information up to date.

HOW THE TAPE FORMATS DIFFER

Different tape formats have been evolving ever since video started to be developed in the 1950s. The formats are distinguished principally by the width of the tape itself, the size of the cassette, and by the differences in loading between different format VCRs.

VCRs for domestic use record on small-format tape – half-inch or 8mm wide. Half-inch is represented by VHS, which is the most popular format, and Betamax. 8mm is a newer format, which is attracting much interest as a format for the programme maker because of its light weight and very small size.

> You cannot play different format tapes on one VCR. Eg only VHS tapes can be played on a VHS VCR. You *can*, however, copy from one format to another, provided you have two VCRs and the necessary tapes and cables.

VHS has long been the market leader in small format video. Developed by JVC, it soon outstripped the Philips 1500 system, which was the first colour small-format cassette video on the domestic market. Philips developed another format, the V2000 range, but again failed to make a significant in-road into the home market. Both these Philips formats have been discontinued, and Philips have now added their name to the VHS range and 8mm.

VHS is now also available in physically smaller cassettes, which have been developed to enable smaller machines to be used for video. These use identical VHS tape to standard size VHS, but have a shorter tape length. They can be replayed on standard VHS VCRs by loading the VHS-C cassette into a special empty caddy which is the same size as a standard VHS cassette. Newer VHS machines with HQ (high quality) circuitry give even better picture quality.

Betamax was developed by Sony, and is a small-format version of their U-Matic industrial VCR format. Betamax has never been as popular as VHS, and Betamax separate portable systems have all been discontinued, leaving only camcorders. However one wonders how long Sony can continue to support two small-format video systems, given the increasing popularity of the 8mm format.

8mm is the most recent format, and looks set to rival the two other small-format contenders. Quality of sound and pictures matches VHS and Betamax, and 8mm has the added attraction of a far smaller, lighter VCR, making it particularly suitable for portable location use. For the Hi-Fi buff, this is the only format which has digital sound on its top range mains-only VCRs.

HOW TO CHOOSE A FORMAT

All these tape formats have their merits and drawbacks. In terms of quality and features for shooting video, all are perfectly acceptable. Choosing a format is largely a matter of personal choice. Price, portability, compatibility with an existing system, design, availability – some or all of these will affect which one you choose. The features available between the different formats are broadly similar. However you will generally find less features available on camcorders than on separate camera and portable VCR systems.

At all times, try not to let the technical aspects get out of control. Remember that you can record, and make interesting programmes, with a camera no matter what VCR you have. Enjoyable programmes are based on good techniques applied to good ideas. You need only the simplest equipment to make videos which you – and others – will enjoy watching.

CONTROLS ON A CAMCORDER (VCR SECTION) AND VCR

Each camcorder and VCR, no matter what the format, operates on the same basic principle – the tape cassette is loaded into the machine, and you then have a choice of operations. Most of these operations are common to all camcorders and VCRs, some are found only on certain models within a manufacturer's range.

Pause   When the tape is in Play mode, it is scanned 50 times a second, to 'read' the information recorded on it, and replay it on your TV. Whilst playing, you can pause to examine a still frame. Pause can also be used during record, between shots. Pause should not be used for long periods, as the continual contact between the record and playback heads and one part of the tape will soon clog them up, and wear the tape out.

Rewind and Fast Forward   When you decide you want to play a different part of the tape, Rewind or Fast Forward can be used. When either of these controls is selected on VHS or 8mm, the tape unlaces from the VCR, and the tape is wound backwards or forwards at high speed. This is for finding different parts of a recording quickly.

Picture Search   There are two important problems in finding different parts of a recording quickly. First, because the tape is unlaced from the VCR for this operation, it is not possible to see the picture whilst Rewind or Fast Forward are taking place. Second, because of the high speed at which Rewind and Fast Forward take place, it is difficult to cue the tape precisely to find the start of the sequence you want.

Picture Search overcomes both these problems. Camcorders and VCRs vary, but generally those which have Picture Search allow fast play without sound in both directions – usually at about 7 or 9 times normal speed. This is possible because the tape is kept in contact with the heads during Search. There is some interference on picture during Search, but it is minimal. Search is valuable as it allows fast and accurate cueing of recorded material for playback. This is most useful when cueing up tapes for editing.

Almost all camcorders and VCRs have other controls and features over and above the basic ones. Exactly which depends on the particular model. Some of the extra features are very useful for shooting video, so it is worth taking a little time to read about each one, and then use the checklist when you are choosing a camcorder or VCR to rent or buy.

Remote control   A remote control lets you operate the camcorder or VCR from a distance, either by direct wired connection, or by infra-red signals. These have an important function apart from allowing you to operate from the armchair. When on location, there may be occasions when you want to control the recording from a distance. A remote control is one way of getting round this problem.

It is also a useful feature when replaying tapes for an audience, especially if you are doing so as part of a talk or lecture. You may not want to distract them by having to reach over to start and stop the tape each time you want to make a point.

You may find difficulties using an infra-red control in sunlight where the full strength of the signal may not get through from the remote control – a wired version is preferable in such circumstances.

Slow motion, frame advance   These are of limited use, and more of a novelty that any real asset. The exception is when you need to slow action down for analysis, such as when going through a football game with the players to illustrate errors in marking, positional play and strategy. You will probably rarely need frame by frame analysis, which advances the action a fraction of a second at a time; so of the two, slow motion is the more useful.

Hi-Fi/stereo, manual audio recording level   Good quality sound is crucial to good programmes. Some mains-only VCRs have stereo Hi-Fi sound channels, in addition to the normal mono audio channel. When shooting video, however, only the linear non Hi-Fi sound channel is used.

Some Hi-Fi VCRs offer the facility to make Hi-Fi audio-only recordings which vie with audio cassettes for quality – and having longer possible recording times. Note that all Hi-Fi recordings can only be played back as Hi-Fi on Hi-Fi VCRs.

A standard feature on all mains-only Hi-Fi VCRs is manual audio recording level. This is well worth having. It gives you control over the level of the sound you are recording onto tape, and will defeat the automatic level control, sometimes called automatic gain control (AGC). This is a poor feature for the programme maker, as different audio sources are artificially evened out, and background noise is increased when sound levels are low.

Manual control also enables you to fade audio in and out at the beginning and end of each recording. By fading up sound at the beginning of each recording, you can avoid recording the click which sometimes occurs when the tape starts.

Hi-Fi VCRs also have audio level meters, which give a visual idea of the sound recording level as you are shooting the scene.

Noise reduction is another feature to look out for. This reduces the hiss which can be a problem on recordings using narrow audio tracks.

Back-space edit   Back-space editing allows you to assemble a number of recordings without picture roll or 'glitches' on vision between them. This interference can be quite distracting, lasting several seconds. Clean edits will give a much more professional look to your programmes. However back-space editing only works if the machine has *not* been put via the Stop mode before shooting the next sequence. In other words, for back-space editing to operate during recordings, the pause control must be operated between each sequence. Back-space editing cues up the second recording a fraction before the end of the first, to give a clean transition from one scene to another.

Insert edit   Insert edit allows you to replace part of a recording with new pictures from a camera or another VCR, leaving clean cuts at the 'Edit In' and 'Edit Out' points.

Video In and Out sockets   These should be used for editing, and to make higher quality tape copies than are possible using the antenna connection. They are also used to replay on a monitor or TV with audio and video (AV) inputs. It also means that you can use a higher quality camera with your VCR should you want to upgrade your system, or to hire one for a special purpose.

Some mains-only VCRs are now fitted with a Euroconnector (also called PERITEL), which is a single multi-way plug for AV, combining Audio and Video In *and* Out.

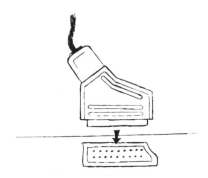

A Euroconnector (PERITEL) is fitted to some VCRs and TVs for replay using pure video and audio.

Audio dub   Audio dub is used to replace the existing sound track on a videotape with a new sound track. On Hi-Fi VCRs, which have two stereo audio tracks as well as the normal audio track, audio dub replaces the normal audio track only, as the Hi-Fi tracks are separately recorded with the video track.

On some VCRs, the normal audio track is split into two half-width audio tracks (stereo), and audio dub can be used to replace one half-track only. This allows mixing of two soundtracks, say live sound and a voice-over, without two-machine editing or separate sound mixing. Audio levels can be tricky to gauge though, as the original live sound on the half-track will be at reduced level when the new half-track is dubbed on.

Headphone socket   Some models incorporate a small sound amplifier with which you can monitor sound level and quality with headphones or an earpiece. You can check that sound is being recorded at all, and to a required standard.

Long-play   This is a feature which should not be used for programme making. It slows recording and playback to half-speed, doubling the recording and playback time of tapes, but the quality of reproduction is not as good as normal play. Recordings made in Long Play cannot be played on conventional VCRs which do not have Long Play.

Real-time tape counter   All camcorders and VCRs have digital tape counters, which are useful for locating recorded material for playback. But real-time tape counters are doubly useful, as they can be used to find a sequence when playing a tape back on any VCR with a real-time tape counter. One number advances every second, to show exactly how long the recording is in actual time. Ordinary tape counters do not work to minutes and seconds, are not very accurate, and usually vary between one machine and the next, which makes finding recordings difficult when replaying a tape on a different machine.

The most important feature of all   It is, of course, picture and sound quality. Not the manufacturer's quoted figures at the back of the instruction book, but quality as you, the user, can see and hear. Too many people fail to check out camcorders and VCRs before investing their money. Always make test recordings, and play them back, checking that the picture and sound are as good as you would want.

21

VCR CHECKLIST

This list covers the features relevant to making videos, and which are not found on all VCRs. Decide which features you want, and grade them 1, 2 or 3 according to importance. Then compare for quality the models which have the features you require. The camcorder checklist follows the camera section.

Format
HQ circuitry
Hi-Fi sound
Noise reduction
Audio dub
Remote control
Real-time tape counter
Video In and Out sockets
Insert edit
Slow motion
Long play
Back-space editing

VCR make & model:
Price:
Supplier:
Quality rating (1 to 10):

CONTROLS ON A CAMCORDER (CAMERA SECTION) AND CAMERA

As with VCRs, quality is the most important factor in choosing a camcorder and camera. There are, of course, other criteria – availability, price, weight, type of viewfinder, extra features – but picture quality is paramount. The technology of small-format video is now so advanced that real differences in quality can be distinguished between one camcorder or camera, and another.

When judging quality, use the camcorder or camera in the kind of environment where you'll be doing most of your work. It's no use trying it out under the bright fluorescent or tungsten-halogen spot lamps in the dealer's showroom when you need a system which works well in low light. Try to arrange to hire the one you like for the weekend, so that you can put it through its paces under proper test conditions. Note how easy it is (a) to operate the controls while recording, and (b) to keep it still when hand-holding.

Tube or microchip   Tube camcorders and cameras share the disadvantage of being fragile and sensitive to burns from bright light sources. Microchip camcorders can be made far smaller than tube camcorders and can be pointed at the brightest spotlights, or even the sun, without damage. The same applies to cameras. A charge-coupled device (CCD) or metal oxide semi-conductor (MOS) imager replaces the conventional tube.

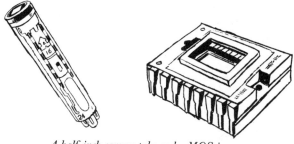

A half-inch camera tube and a MOS imager.

Many experienced camera operators prefer the better stability of a heavier, bulkier camera than many currently available. Because tube cameras are more sensitive to light, they also tend to work better in low light conditions than do microchip cameras. Tube camcorders and cameras are prone to image-lag. This is a ghosting or after-image which is visible on the screen after panning across a light source such as a candle or light bulb. It can be some seconds before the after-image disappears. Microchip camcorders and cameras are free from this.

Viewfinder   Most camcorders and cameras are fitted with an electronic viewfinder as standard. This is a small monochrome monitor fitted to the side of the camera, which not only allows you to monitor what you are shooting accurately, but also enables you to view playback. Optical viewfinders are less satisfactory. They employ lenses rather than electronics, and are therefore less accurate. Also, they do not offer playback on location. Viewfinders tend to carry a number of warning lights, such as tape running, low battery and light level warnings.

Focus ring   The focus ring is the part of the lens furthest from the camcorder or camera body, and is used to get a sharp picture – in focus. Focussing is achieved by turning the ring one way or the other until the picture is sharp. This can be checked using the electronic viewfinder, if fitted. However, where you can, it is easier to use a regular TV or monitor. Unless your eyesight and the ambient lighting are both good, it is not easy to focus and frame shots in a tiny viewfinder. This is why studio cameras have larger viewfinders fitted.

Auto-focus can be useful. However, the auto-focus cannot take decisions – it will focus on the main subject in the frame, so you must make sure that you can over-ride it where necessary. Also be warned that the auto-focus draws a lot of power which, if you are using batteries, will soon drain them.

All focussing should be done with the lens in the largest close up position possible; always zoom in before you focus.

Zoom lens The vast majority have a zoom lens fitted as standard. This enables you to select many different shot types ranging from extreme close-up to very long shot. Most zoom lenses also have a Macro setting, which enables focussing on flat objects, eg printed matter, at very close range. This is invaluable for using printed, graphic and other text or pictorial matter, where the regular focal settings of the lens would not focus.

The zoom lens is always used in focussing. Zoom in to the biggest close-up of the subject, and then focus. The subject will now stay in focus throughout the whole zoom range, for all shots. If the subject moves, or you move, re-focussing will be necessary. Once you have selected a shot, leave the zoom alone unless there is good reason. Many initial efforts at programme making are spoilt because the zoom lens is used too enthusiastically. It is disturbing to the eye of the viewer to seem to move constantly into and out of a shot; after all, zooming is unnatural – the human eye cannot zoom.

There is usually a choice between manual and electric control of the zoom. Which you use is a matter of personal preference. Some find it much easier to get a smooth zoom using the electric option. Note that, like the auto-focus, the electric zoom will quickly drain your batteries.

Iris Iris is another name for aperture. Its size has to be varied according to the amount of available light. In poor light, the iris needs to be wide open, so that you get enough light to the tube or microchip for a reasonable image.

Unfortunately, when the iris is wide open, focussing becomes very critical. The area which can be in focus at one time is called the depth of field. The depth of field gets narrower the smaller the iris setting. The iris ring has numbers on it, like a stills camera. These are 'f' numbers, which can be used as a guide to the aperture setting. The widest iris setting is generally f1.8, the narrowest f22. Therefore, the rule of thumb is, the more light the better – for focussing and for a brighter, crisper shot. A picture gain control, when fitted, increases the sensitivity of the camera, which is useful in low light. But its use will make the picture quality more grainy.

Auto-iris is standard on all models, but again check that manual override is available for shots where you may want to deliberately over-expose or under-expose.

Auto-fade up and **auto-fade out** automatically opens and closes the iris when required. This is easier than turning the iris ring by hand.

Back light compensation (BLC) adjusts the aperture setting when shooting against a bright background, for example a window. If you shoot against a window, the auto-iris will close. BLC will over-expose the window area, thus allowing, for example, a person to be correctly exposed. Without BLC, such a shot can look 'bleached'.

Microphone Built-in microphones are more of a hindrance than a benefit. They are poor quality, in the wrong place for optimum sound recordings, and will pick up adjustments to focus and zoom etc. When you want to use a separate microphone, plugging it in the camcorder or camera will automatically disarm the built-in microphone.

White balance control The human eye can make compensations for different types of light – daylight, fluorescent, tungsten-halogen, etc, so that objects remain essentially the same colour to us when the light changes. Camcorders and cameras have to be programmed to cope with such changes to give accurate colour reproduction in any given light.

Whenever you change location, you must remember to set the white balance, or your colours will be unnatural. Check adjustment, where you can, on a good quality colour TV or monitor, and take special note of flesh tones, grass, buses, etc, which must be correctly represented.

A few camcorders and cameras have continually self-adjusting auto-white balance; if you use this facility, don't neglect to check the colour balance visually, too, with a colour TV or monitor.

Also there is sometimes a colour balance control, which allows some fine adjustment of white balance towards the red (artificial light) or blue (daylight) ends of the spectrum.

Lighting selection   Some cameras have switchable selection for different types of light. These are very good, and enable more faithful reproduction of colour.

Trigger   A trigger is used to start and stop a camcorder. Separate systems using compatible multi-way cable can be operated from the camera or the VCR. When using the trigger take care not to nudge the camcorder or camera by mistake. This will be particularly noticeable in large close-ups, where even the slightest movement will be exaggerated.

Multi-way cable   The multi-way cable is the 'umbilical cord' between camera and VCR. It carries ten or more wires, each of which have their own function. Manufacturers being manufacturers, the connectors at the end of these are not always compatible with other makes of VCR. However, adaptors are available, although you may not be able to have all the camera functions if you use a different make VCR. You may find yourself without warning lamps or trigger operation, for example. Trigger polarity reversal switches sometimes get round this problem.

Take good care of this cable. The wires it contains are quite slender, and each is separately soldered to its own terminal. Avoid kinks in it, or pulling on it, which could easily lead to failure at a critical moment.

Extensions are available, which are valuable in allowing you to use the camera more freely some distance away from the VCR. However they are quite expensive. Do not attempt to use more than two standard extension cables together, as the signal will weaken and give you an unstable picture.

Tripod mounting   The tripod mounting is simply a standard screw thread at the base of the camcorder or camera. On some cameras, it is at the base of the pistol grip. Make sure that the tripod is screwed into the camera to its fullest extent before tightening the locking ring. Screw the bush into the camera, not the other way round; avoid twisting the camera cable at all times.

Extra features on camcorders and cameras make a hefty difference to price. Think whether you really need them before making your choice.

Titling Electronic titling is a feature limited by the quality of graphics it generates. These are 'teletext' type, which are really too spindly to provide quality graphic displays. Apart from this major problem, there are a wide range of colours and effects available, including superimposition, memory and call-up, status check on viewfinder or monitor/TV, zoom, stopwatch and date.

Auto-fade Some cameras have auto-fade in and out to use at the beginning and end of programmes. This is useful if you have difficulty in operating the iris ring smoothly. Cameras without this feature, but with auto-iris, can achieve an auto-fade in by framing and focussing up on your shot, manually closing the iris, and then switching to auto-iris.

Negaposi switch This enables negative stills film to be viewed and recorded as a positive, ie in normal colour.

CAMERA CHECKLIST

This covers the main features you might want in a camera for making video movies. Decide which features you want and grade them 1, 2 or 3 according to importance. Then compare for quality the models which have the features you require.

Ease of operation
Tube
CCD/MOS
Electronic viewfinder
Auto-focus
Electric zoom
Auto-iris (manual override)
Picture gain
Built-in microphone
Titling
Lighting selection
Auto-white
Auto-fade
Negaposi switch

Camera make & model:
Price:
Supplier:
Quality rating (1 to 10):

CAMCORDER CHECK LIST

This covers the main features you might want in a camcorder for making movies. Decide which features you want, and grade them 1, 2 or 3 according to importance. Then compare for quality the models which have the features you require.

Ease of operation
Format
Tube
CCD/MOS
Record only
Record and replay
Audio dub
Remote control
Real time tape counter
Insert edit
Slow motion
Long play
Picture search
Back-space editing
Electronic viewfinder
Full focussing
Auto-focus
Zoom lens
Electric zoom
Auto-iris (manual override)
Built-in microphone
Titling
Lighting selection
Auto-fade
Negaposi switch
Tuner-timer available

Camcorder make & model:
Price:
Supplier:
Quality rating (1 to 10):

HOW TO GET A TRUE PICTURE USING FILTERS AND WHITE BALANCE

Getting a good picture is important whether you are using a camcorder or a separate camera. The electronics of your video system are very sophisticated, and packed full of minituarised circuitry. To make the best use of your equipment, you must be prepared to set it up properly.

If there is a light selection switch, it will be switchable between artificial light and daylight. Daylight and artificial light are different in colour. This is measured in degrees Kelvin (°K) which is a measure of colour temperature. Bright sunlight has the highest colour temperature, varying between about 5000 and 8000°K; the light is blue in colour.

The lowest colour temperature you will probably need to work in is inside using ordinary light bulbs. Fluorescent lighting is a stronger light, with a higher colour temperature. So once you have selected the indoor or outdoor filter setting, there will still be differences in the colour temperature of your lighting. You have to set the white balance control of the camera to compensate for differences in lighting, or colours will not look natural.

A camera with continuously self-adjusting white balance will self-adjust if, for example, the sun goes behind clouds whilst you are shooting. Others without this facility must be set for each new location. Adjustment of these is straightforward. Select the correct light setting, and switch on any extra lighting you intend to use. Place a sheet of white paper or card where the main subject will be.

From the shooting position, fill the viewfinder with a close-up of the white paper or card. Defocus, and press the white balance switch for five seconds. The white balance is now set *for that lighting*. Remember, if you don't have continuously adjusting white balance, that you must re-set the white balance if the light changes, or if the subject moves into brighter or darker light. If you shoot inside using a daylight setting, you will get orange pictures; if you shoot outside using an indoor setting, you will get blue pictures. Any adjustment, with a manual colour balance control, should be done using a good TV or colour monitor for reference.

Many camcorders and cameras have an LED check light in the electronic viewfinder which will confirm whether white balance has been correctly set or not. But if you can, using a colour monitor or TV, check visually that the setting is correct. The best way to do this is to ask the subject to stand in shot once you have set the white balance, and check for accurate flesh tones. Don't forget, though, that the TV or monitor *must* be properly adjusted for colour, contrast and brightness, if it is going to be used to monitor colour quality.

If you are not happy with the colour balance, for example if the colours look 'muddy', it may well be that more light is required. This could apply especially to CCD and MOS imagers which need more light than conventional tube cameras. If the colours 'bleed' into each other, then you are using too much light – either switch to manual aperture control and stop down, or use less lighting. If this happens in bright sunlight, use a neutral density (ND) filter, which will filter out the harshness of very bright sunlight, which is a common problem in sunny holiday resorts.

When you are working inside, use the daylight setting if you are only working with natural light. Once you add artificial light, say by switching on ordinary room lights, or adding a video lamp, you may have colour balancing problems. Although the human eye can easily cope with and adjust to different strengths and intensities of light, video cannot. So a mix of light of different temperatures may not allow the camera to set correctly. One solution if you need to mix light is to place an orange gel over the windows; this effectively converts daylight to the lower colour temperature of artificial lights. A blue gel over spotlights will raise their temperature towards that of daylight.

The range of lens filters available for video is fairly limited at present, but any stills photography filter can be used. If it doesn't fit your lens mount, and you haven't got an adaptor, simply jam it into the lens hood. Ones you may find useful are infra-red for clear long-distance shots, and polarising filters for shots where there is a problem of light reflecting off water.

All effects filters will reduce the amount of light through the lens, so unless lighting is good their effect will be partial or lost altogether.

HOW TO CONNNECT UP THE POWER SUPPLY

VCRs are powered by batteries or mains. Internal batteries are supplied by the manufacturer as accessories. You can also get separate heavy duty battery belts or packs which will require an adaptor or specially wired connector. When buying a battery, take the exact model number of your machine with you, and the dealer should be able to provide you with a battery which has the right connector. A safer, though perhaps less convenient, alternative is to take your equipment with you to buy all accessories such as batteries, and try it out in the shop to make sure it works.

If you are using a mains-only VCR, then there will be a mains lead either going straight inside the VCR, or to a mains connector which will push into a main socket, usually at the back of the VCR. There is usually also an on – off switch at the back, and there may also be a standby switch at the front. Once connected, a mains-only VCR is usually left with the plug socket switched on so that the digital clock stays on for automatic recording of TV programmes. The front standby switch need only be on when the VCR is recording or playing.

Portable VCRs can be powered from the mains in two ways. The most common is a tuner-timer which also serves as a mains adaptor for the VCR and a charger for the VCR battery. For some VCRs you can get a unit which is just a mains adaptor and charger, without the tuner-timer facility. This is obviously cheaper as well as being more portable, and would be useful, for example, if you already had a standard mains-only VCR and therefore did not need a second tuner-timer.

In both the above cases, the portable VCR is not connected directly to the mains; the mains lead plugs into the tuner-timer or mains adaptor. Attached to the tuner-timer or mains adaptor you will find a cable which connects to the portable VCR; the socket is usually marked 'DC 12v in', standing for 'Direct current, 12 volts in'.

You may have guessed that because the mains current is reduced to 12 volts to power a portable VCR, it is possible to use a car battery. Correct, but check the voltage carefully, as not all are 12 volts. You will need a special lead which is wired to connect to the cigarette lighter socket in the car dashboard. Bear in mind that on some cars, notably the safety conscious Swedish Saabs and Volvos, the cigarette lighter circuit does not operate if the ignition is not switched on. This is to try to prevent small children causing a fire or burning themselves when left in an unattended car. In this case, the engine would have to be running to power the VCR, or you would soon have a flat battery. You connect the lead from the cigarette lighter socket to the same DC in socket on the portable VCR. You should use a special lead with a voltage stabiliser in it, just in case the car is started and the regulator is faulty.

Camcorders are powered from batteries in the same way as portable VCRs. Don't be afraid to ignore the manufacturers' own batteries if they're not offered as inclusive in the price you pay. Better to pay two or three times as much for a high power battery belt or pack which will give you much more than treble the recording and playback time.

Most, but not all, camcorders can be used with tuner-timers and have an RF out adaptor to enable direct playback to a TV set, or tape copying. So think carefully about all your video needs, including whether you want to use the system for off-air recording, copying and editing, before you finally commit yourself. Mains operation of camcorders is via a mains adaptor. This is sometimes used for charging batteries too, while some battery chargers are separate.

A battery belt or pack will give several times more power than the internal battery.

HOW TO CONNECT A SEPARATE CAMERA TO A VCR

In straightforward cases, where a camera is being used with a same-make portable recorder, the camera will link direct to the VCR via a single multi-way cable, which will carry video and sound from camera to recorder and also power the camera. As far as camcorders are concerned, camera and recorder are a single integral unit and cannot be separated.

If you are using a different make camera with a portable VCR, or any camera with a mains-only VCR, mains operated camera adaptors are readily available to connect any camera to any VCR.

Some cameras at the top of the domestic range, and all cameras designed for industrial and professional work, have their own separate power supply, as well as the option of taking power from the VCR. These can be connected direct to most VCRs by a standard 75 Ohm video cable. Connectors are usually BNC type (see diagram on p. 82). However, adaptors and adaptor leads are available from good video shops to convert and connect one kind of video connector to another.

If you are using a camera which has a separate video output as well as the usual multi-way camera to VCR lead, then it is possible to use a long video cable, which gives you the freedom to roam around with the camera away from the VCR. The multi-way cable extensions, which would enable you to do the same thing, are extremely expensive, whereas ordinary video cable is not. Remember, though, that you will have to make separate arrangements for sound. The microphone will have to be plugged directly into the VCR as the video cable will not carry audio signals as well. But connecting the microphone separately is advisable in any case for quality reasons, whichever way you connect camera to VCR.

HOW TO USE A TELEVISION WITH A VIDEO SYSTEM

Any TV can be used to play back video pictures and sound. To set up playback, disconnect the lead to the TV aerial from the back of the TV and connect a short antenna lead from the TV to the video RF Out adaptor. For recording and viewing TV programmes connect the TV aerial lead to the video RF In adaptor.

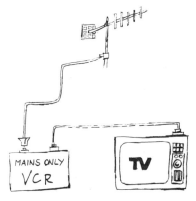

How to connect a mains-only VCR to a TV.

Most mains-only VCRs can generate a test signal which will show on the TV when it is correctly tuned to the VCR. The screen will be divided into black and white segments. The tuning control of a TV is usually situated under a panel at the front of the set. To tune, select an unused channel on the TV. If the first four channels are tuned to BBC 1, BBC 2, ITV and Channel 4, you may as well use the fifth channel.

Having connected up the VCR, switch on the test signal on the VCR. Tune the channel control until the picture is sharp and clear.

Be sure to tune into the strongest, clearest signal. There will be signals from other regions, and 'ghost' signals, which will have more interference. Now the VCR is correctly tuned you can switch off the test signal, and you will now be able to use the TV to play back from the VCR.

If you are using the TV to look at the picture from your camera whilst recording, this is called 'monitoring' – you monitor the shot on the larger screen. Do not confuse this with a monitor which is used to play back video pictures and sound with better quality than is possible on an ordinary TV set.

If your mains-only VCR cannot generate a test signal, or you are using a portable, then simply frame a shot in the viewfinder of the camera, or play back a tape, and then tune in the TV to that signal.

TVs do go out of tune, and you will notice this by distortion of picture or sound or both. If it happens, retune the TV as above. Some TVs have an automatic frequency control (AFC), which should be switched off when tuning, and on when the set is tuned.

For playing back videos, the smaller the TV screen the better the quality of the pictures will be. A large screen will only serve to highlight any poor contrast or colour, so where you can, play back on a small screen. If you have to play a tape to a large number of people, try using two TVs with an RF splitter box to take the signal to each set. To play back on more than two TV sets you should use a signal amplifier to boost the signal for each set, as the signal is weakened by each split of the signal.

Better quality is possible by linking a chain of sets with both A/V In and Out sockets (see pp. 90–92).

It is important to adjust colour, brightness and contrast controls carefully, particularly when you are using a TV to gauge the quality of the camera picture as far as white balance and aperture are concerned. When you have made all the adjustments, point the camera at someone's face; this is the easiest way to spot any inaccuracies.

During video recording with a TV connected it is essential to have the volume control turned right down to avoid a screeching noise called howl-round, or audio feedback. This is caused by sound passing from loudspeaker to microphone in a never-ending loop until the system overloads.

It is also a bad idea to point tube camcorders and cameras directly at the TV screen when recording. This gives the effect which is the video equivalent of audio feedback, called video feedback. Although the visual effect is quite fascinating when it is first seen, the looping of the video image between camcorder and screen intensifies it each time, and you could well end up burning the camcorder tube.

A battery-operated TV will allow you to monitor and playback on location away from the mains, and will certainly be easier to use to set up shots than the viewfinder. But it is better to opt for a portable monitor which can accept pure video and audio signals from the VCR or camcorder. If you want a battery-operated TV anyway, there are good battery-operated combined TV/monitors available. And you have the bonus of enhancing the quality of your programmes by playing them back on a small screen.

LOOKING AFTER YOUR VIDEO EQUIPMENT

There is a lot you can do to look after your equipment to prolong its life. If you use your equipment frequently it is worthwhile taking it to a local dealer for regular servicing. This will include checking the factory settings of the camera, and cleaning the video heads. It is possible to clean heads yourself using one of the kits available, but it is even easier to make a hash of it and end up paying for a new set of video heads! Unless you are sure what you are doing, leave it to the experts.

Dirty video heads are hard to avoid. In the worst cases, you will either lose all, or part of, the picture when replaying tapes. A temporary cure may be to use the search control until the picture returns. This partially cleans the heads, and may return your picture until it is convenient to have the heads properly cleaned. Don't use the various types of video tape head cleaning tapes. These work by being played like a normal tape for a couple of seconds, but the special tape is so abrasive that it is very easy to damage the heads using it. Why risk such high precision equipment for the sake of a few pounds spent on regular servicing to get the job done properly?

If your lens gets dusty, use a proper photographic airbrush. You can get one from any good photographic shop, and they are not expensive at all. Never use handkerchiefs or tissues which can easily scratch the surface of the lens.

If you should accidentally point a tube at the sun, or a bright light, or if you leave it pointing at a light area too long and a mark appears on the picture, it will be burnt. As soon as you spot it, switch the camcorder on, and point the lens at a bright, evenly lit area, like a wall. If the burn is not too bad this salvage operation might make it disappear after a short while. If not, you'll need a new tube, as the mark will appear on every shot you record.

Tube camcorders and cameras should not really be pointed directly down. Particles of dust within the tube when it is manufactured can fall onto the 'target' or 'tubeface' and will cause white spots on the picture.

Such faults as occur with video equipment can often be attributed either to user error, such as incorrect setting of white balance or switches in the wrong position, or faulty leads and connectors. Antenna leads will give problems if the inner and outer wires touch, as will pure video and audio leads if the wiring is not in order. Use a simple battery-operated circuit tester to test that the wires of leads are properly separated from each other.

Rough handling of leads and connectors can cause them to become loose and thus unreliable. Soldering must be done with care, as the connectors used with video are quite tiny. If in doubt about your own ability to make up or repair a lead, buy one ready made. If you are in London, the shops in Tottenham Court Road and Edgware Road stock every lead you could possibly need; otherwise your local video stockist may be able to help, or at least get them for you. For audio requirements, you will probably do better to visit a good music shop rather than a video dealer who often carry limited stocks of microphones, leads and audio accessories.

The push in/pull out microphone connectors common on video equipment are a frequent source of trouble. As the connectors and sockets become worn, the fit gets looser, and it is quite easy for the plug to become accidentally disconnected during recording. This can, of course, ruin your recording and your reputation all in one. To lessen the chances of it happening to you, wind the lead twice, loosely, around a handle or the tripod before plugging into the microphone socket. Then, if the lead is pulled during recording, the plug will stay in place.

When working on mains power you may experience a phenomenon known as mains hum, which is a humming sound audible on playback of recorded material. To avoid the audio circuits picking up stray and unwanted sound from the mains supply many professionals use battery power only, when recording on video – you could do worse than follow their example.

Batteries require careful attention if they are to continue working efficiently during their life. Like car batteries, video batteries don't last for ever, and the older they get the greater the chance that they will let you down. Most portable VCRs and camcorders work with nickel-cadmium (Ni-Cad) batteries. To make them last as long as they should, these must be fully discharged before recharging. Battery level warning lamps light up shortly before the battery runs out. They should be stored discharged, although every few months they should be charged and discharged. Lead acid batteries, on the other hand, must be stored charged and should not be allowed to run right down, or they'll not work any more. Lead acid batteries should be re-charged as soon as possible after use.

If you take a camcorder or VCR from a cold atmosphere to a warm one – eg from the boot of the car into a centrally heated room – it will not work. Condensation will have formed inside the machine which would cause the tape to stick around the drum when loaded up. A built-in sensor, where fitted, will detect any condensation and cut out all circuits until the condensation has disappeared. Using a hairdryer, whilst dealing effectively with the condensation, may also warp the cassette housing or cause other damage. It is best to allow enough time when moving equipment from location to location for it to acclimatise; half an hour is usually more than enough time.

The condensation cut-out may also operate when you try to play or record a tape in damp conditions. However, it is not uncommon for video to continue working satisfactorily in the most appalling conditions of heat, cold, dust and damp but it does make sense to protect both camera and recorder when working outside. Very cold batteries will not give all their normal power – rather like a cold car battery. Take a large golfing umbrella on location, and buy an inexpensive soft padded holdall-type bag which will carry and protect all your equipment.

IF THE CAMERA OR CAMCORDER WON'T WORK

If you suddenly lose power for no apparent reason check the obvious things first, like the connection of the battery or mains supply. Is the battery fully charged? Check the fuse in the plug.

There is also a micro fuse inside, which you might try changing if you have a spare. If you are using infra-red remote control be wary of sunlight falling on the sensor panel, which might cause the recorder to stop suddenly during a recording.

If you can't get a picture, check that the aperture is open, and that all connectors are firmly in place. If there is a tuner-timer, it should be switched off. VCRs should be switched to camera or auxiliary input, not TV. If the camera has a power save or standby switch check that that is in the correct position. On some VCRs the record button needs to be pressed before the camera will work. If you still can't get a picture, unscrew the camera cable which attaches to the VCR, and check that all the wires are firmly connected. If you are using a camera extension lead, remove it and try the camera lead directly into the VCR.

You have, of course, taken the lens cap off the camera . . .?

The most common mistake that beginners make when shooting with video is to forget to press Pause at the end of a sequence. So when they want to record the next sequence and press Pause again, instead of the VCR starting up, it stops. The result is lots of shots of peoples' feet!

If you have a VCR running light in the viewfinder check that it's on when you're recording; alternatively, check that the tape is actually moving.

ESSENTIAL ACCESSORIES

A microphone   First on the list is a good quality microphone. Although most cameras and camcorders come with built-in microphones they are generally poor quality. Added to this, they will pick up any vibration, hand movement, camera operation, etc, whilst recording. Furthermore, the microphone position is always wrong when using a built-in microphone. The ideal position is as near as possible to the subject so that sound has as much 'presence' and life as possible. Using a built-in microphone, the sound will be tinny and distant.

Once you have tried a quality separate microphone, you will never want to use a built-in one again. The difference is quite astonishing. But it *is* more inconvenient, in that you will have to think about a cable and positioning the microphone on a stand or getting someone to hold it. If the cable is really a problem, consider getting a radio microphone system which uses a mini transmitter and receiver to pass the audio signals to VCR. These are more expensive, of course, but extremely useful in all sorts of situations.

The microphone can be plugged directly into the camcorder microphone socket, and into either the camera or VCR on separate systems. Check that you have the correct plug – generally a mini jack is used. Make sure that the built-in microphone is disconnected whichever way you connect a microphone, or the separate microphone may not work. For outdoor work get a foam rubber windshield to place over the head of the microphone. This will help to prevent wind noises; be warned, even the slightest breeze will sound like a force 10 gale when passing across the face of a sensitive microphone.

A hand-held omni-directional microphone is the best sort to go for. It will pick up sound evenly from varying distances from the subject, which makes it very versatile. It is less susceptible to wind noise than a uni-directional one. It can be used in all sorts of different situations, including interviews, presentations, voice-overs, commentaries and discussions. Other microphones are more specialist, though no less useful.

Hand-held microphones must be able to reproduce a wide variation of voice frequencies, as they are used both close to mouth and at arm's length, and for loud and soft voices. Electret condenser, or battery microphones tend to give a better frequency response, and are more sensitive in use.

Some microphones have an on-off switch which you must remember to switch on before recording.

Headphones Headphones are essential to monitor the presence and quality of sound on to videotape. Good sound quality is crucial to good video and the only way to check that the microphone is correctly set and working is to use headphones. An earpiece is a lower quality substitute, which *will* confirm that you are recording sound, but not much more.

Monitoring the sound continually whilst recording video is also the only way to be sure that the microphone has not suddenly become disconnected or developed a fault. You don't need an expensive pair, and those designed for sound systems are fine – the lighter the better though, if you're going to wear them for long periods at a time. Check the plug is compatible with your VCR or camcorder; usually a minijack is needed.

A tripod   Only hand-hold your camcorder or camera for a good reason, such as if you want an unusually high angle, or you need to move (track) with the subject, or you deliberately want a particular effect, such as in a chase sequence where the camera movement bobbing up and down whilst moving along adds to the realism. But the lighter your camcorder or camera, the more difficult it will be to hold it steady. So at all other times, to ensure that your shots are as steady as possible, use a tripod.

There are many different sorts available, and at a pinch any will do, but for preference use the heaviest, most solid one you can. The more solid the tripod, the more chance that your shots will be steady and your camera movements smooth. The best have a fluid head which acts as a damping device, giving controlled resistance and therefore smoothness to each camera movement. There are, however, good 'fluid effect' tripods available which are a reasonable compromise. If you do much work inside, then you might find a dolly useful – a mount with wheels for the tripod which makes it easy to move the camera and tripod in any direction between shots and, if necessary, during a shot.

Set up the tripod before you attach the camcorder or camera. To get it level, adjust the height with the legs closed – that way it is easy to get them all the same length. This is much quicker than struggling with the tripod with the legs splayed open. On uneven ground, start with the legs level and make adjustments gradually until the tripod is secure and level.

You will find that there is a metal bush on the tripod, which has a plastic knurled locking wheel outside it. Unscrew the plastic wheel all the way, and then attach the camcorder or camera, tightening the bush as tight as you can with your fingers. Then tighten the locking wheel. Don't let the camcorder or camera crash down: always tighten the tilt head, which controls up and down movement, whenever it is unattended.

A case or bag   Many camcorders are offered for sale complete with a hard case, which provides a good protection. It also provides a good invitation to theft. Disguise it by putting the case in a holdall. If you do not have a hard case, then a padded holdall is as good. You can easily sew in a lining and pad it out with polystyrene chips or thick felt. Many camcorders will fit into a handbag or briefcase.

Alternatively, aluminium flight cases are very durable, if somewhat more expensive. Cut out polystyrene blocks to form secure compartments for the camcorder and all accessories. At the least, any kind of case or bag is better than no protection at all. The important thing is to protect the equipment from mechanical shocks, whilst not drawing attention to the contents.

These accessories are all very useful.

Setting Up
and Basic Techniques

The quality of your recordings will depend to a large extent on how carefully the camcorder or camera has been set up. You should by now be familiar with the controls of your equipment. You've probably noticed that the better the lighting, the better the shot: colours are brighter, and focussing is both easier and sharper. But it is also possible to get quite good quality in low light, but you need to take more care. The camera will be working at its limits, and you will have to set the aperture as wide as possible. The wider the aperture, the smaller the 'f' number, and less of the areas in front of or behind the subject will be in focus.

Are you going to use a tripod, or hand-hold the camcorder or camera? Although these are getting smaller all the time, and there's no doubt that does make them much more convenient and transportable, nevertheless it also makes them difficult to hold steady.

Are you going to use the built-in microphone, or an external one? The built-in one is certainly more convenient, as it's fixed to the camera or camcorder, and there are no trailing cables to worry about. But there is no substitute for having the microphone close to the subject. When it is some distance away, it will pick up a good deal of background noise. Sounds will be rather hollow, and when the subject speaks, the voice will lack 'presence'. This will be particularly unsettling if you happen to have a close-up shot. It won't be very realistic to have the subject appearing to be close to the viewer, while his or her voice appears to be a long way away.

To start with you have to get organised – to make sure that you have everything you need, and to check that everything is working properly. A little time spent in care and attention to details is always well repaid.

ORGANISING AND CHECKING YOUR EQUIPMENT

Apart from your camcorder or camera and VCR, thère will probably be a number of accessories to take on location with you. We've already looked at some of these – a microphone, a tripod, headphones and a bag or case. As you get more ambitious, you may well get a number of others, which will soon seem as indispensable as the videotape you use. You'll also probably have a number of leads and connectors, several videocassettes, and so on.

You'll probably be using your equipment to make recordings of various events and happenings, some of which will be planned, some of which won't. In any event, it's very easy to forget an essential piece of equipment in the excitement and enthusiasm that surrounds some occasions where video is often used – like weddings and holidays, for example. The easiest way to make sure you remember everything is to make out a checklist for all the equipment you'll need to take with you when you go out on location.

It's a good idea to make a lot of copies of this checklist, and then simply tick each piece of equipment off as you load it into your bag or case. Take care to make sure that all batteries you take out with you are fully charged. You can include this as part of your checking procedure. Keep the checklists with your equipment, and to avoid confusion, throw away each copy when you have re-checked that you haven't left anything behind.

LOCATION CHECKLIST

The checklist below is an example only. Adapt it for your own equipment as necessary and remember to update the checklist whenever you buy a new piece of equipment.
Camcorder
2 Batteries (charged?)
2 Videotapes
Tripod
Hand-held microphone
2 Microphone batteries (charged?)
Microphone cable
Spare microphone cable
Microphone cable extension
Headphones
Lens cap
Lens brush
Antenna lead
Masking tape
Screwdriver
Case

Fortunately, video equipment seldom goes wrong. If it does it's likely to be at the most awkward moment. Most faults are fairly minor – leads and connectors working loose. Others can be put down to user error, like forgetting to recharge the batteries, or not setting the white balance properly. But sometimes the problem is more serious, and when this happens it is important to get it seen to as soon as possible.

If you haven't used the equipment for some time, it's as well to check it out before you take it a long distance on location. Connect the camera and recorder together (except camcorders) with the multi-way lead, and put in a battery and a tape. Connect an antenna lead from Video RF Out to the TV, and tune the TV in until you can see a clear picture from the camcorder or camera. Don't forget to take off the lens cap and open the aperture. Adjust the white balance. If you can now see a satisfactory picture on the screen, then all is well. Don't waste any more battery power by using the electric zoom.

When you are simply monitoring the picture like this without recording, it is sometimes called E to E (electronic to electronic), or rehearsal mode. The latter term is more meaningful. It is the mode to use when using the equipment to rehearse shots prior to recording.

Never make the mistake of rehearsing shots with the camcorder or VCR in Record and Pause (or 'standby') mode. You should only use standby when all rehearsing has finished and you are ready to record. This is because in standby mode, the recording head is engaged, with the tape wound tightly round the capstan. Because the heads have to make contact with the tape to scan it, there is minute wear on the tape each time the heads revolve – which they do hundreds of times a minute. If all this is happening on one tiny segment of tape, you will soon wear out that segment completely. Then there will be interference whenever you play back any recording which spans that particular segment of tape. Also as the tape is not moving in standby mode, the heads could clog up as the metal oxide from the tape segment is deposited on them. So always follow the correct procedure: only go to Record and Pause, or standby, when you are ready to record.

Now do a recording and sound check. Connect your microphone to the Microphone In socket, and make a test recording. Proper sentences are better than counting. If you can't think of anything to say, describe what you had for breakfast, or if you didn't have any, what you would have liked to have had! Remember to turn down the sound on the TV while doing this or you will get a nasty howl-round. Now rewind, turn up the TV volume, and play back. Use your eyes and ears to monitor the quality.

Test a microphone by speaking into it. Blowing into it is the quickest way to corrode and ruin a good quality microphone. Also to be avoided are tapping the microphone head with your finger, and bashing it against the palm of your hand. That technique is reserved for pop stars who can afford to buy a new microphone every week!

When packing away, check each piece of equipment off against the checklist. I suggest you put a tick against each item as it is packed away, and another line making a cross when you are packing up at the other end ready to come home.

ON LOCATION

Try to be as organised as possible. You will have to deal with a headphones lead, and perhaps leads for the camera, microphone, and RF to a portable TV as well. It is all too easy to end up with a sprawl of trailing cables, leads and wires. The simple rule is to keep them tidy, but this is easier said than done, especially when you have to make frequent changes of camera position. If you are shooting in a crowded area, then leads cease to become just a nuisance; they can be a positive danger, acting as potential tripwires. In these situations, and especially where children are involved such as at a party, it is essential to keep trailing leads to a minimum. If you can, attach them to the floors or walls with masking tape. Any that are loose can be made more visible by sticking a length of masking tape to the lead.

When sticking masking tape to a lead, turn a couple of inches of tape over and stick it to itself, sticky sides together. This will give you about an inch of tape to wrap around the lead, and the rest of the tape can also be stuck to itself. This avoids leaving a sticky residue on the plastic casing of the lead, which is annoying and difficult to remove.

It is tidier to have cables as short as possible. This also helps to reduce signal loss, and cut out unwanted stray electrical or electronic interference. It's a good idea to have a number of different lengths of extension lead with adaptors in your equipment bag, so that if, for example, you need a longer microphone lead, it can be lengthened as required.

Don't wind leads and cables up tightly, and never wrap the lead around a microphone, as so many novices do. This severely weakens the lead and the connector, and greatly increases the chances of a fault developing. The best way to store away leads is to loop them around your arm loosely, so that the diameter of the loops is about 12 inches. Then secure it with a large rubber band. This will avoid putting any undue strain on the lead or connector, and will also make sure that your leads don't get tangled up when you store them away. Always disconnect plugs and connectors before storing, or in time they will loosen, and the contacts will be weakened.

WHERE TO POSITION THE CAMCORDER OR CAMERA

One of the reasons why making a video is so much fun is that you can be completely creative about what shots you decide to have. By turning the zoom lens you can make the subject appear nearer or further away from the viewer. You can point it wherever you want, have it as high as you want, and change the shot as often as you want. Not surprisingly, a lot of people find this complete freedom a bit daunting. How do you choose a shot? How do you know what the right shot is? Mostly, it's really a matter of common sense.

When you use a camcorder or camera lens, you are using it as the eye of the viewer. The microphone is the ear. The way you use the lens depends on the effect you want to create. If you've a shot of a child, and you want to represent the view of an adult, the lens must be angled to an adult's point of view (POV), that is, downward.

If you deliberately want to make someone look larger than life, then use a low angle – below the eye level of the subject – and point the lens upward. The subject will then appear taller, and possibly more dominant, than they do in real life.

Normally the lens should be set roughly at the eye level of the people you are shooting. If you're recording someone who's standing up, and you're hand-holding, you should also be standing up. If they're sitting down, so should you. If you're using a tripod, that should also be set so that the lens is at the subject's eye level.

Keep the camcorder at the subject's eye level.

So what angle should you use? Here again, common sense will get you a long way. There will be a lot of times when there isn't much choice of angle. If you're stuck in a crowd, for example, that's where you've got to shoot from. If you do have a choice of angle, then the best position will be dictated by what light is available.

In general, you want the strongest light to fall on the subject, so shoot with the light coming from behind you. In a room, for example, the best place is often near the window.

Shoot with your back to the window to make the most use of available light.

Outside, shoot with your back to the sun, unless it is very bright and causing glare or very dark facial shadow, in which case move to the shade. Sometimes finding the best position for the camera may involve quite a bit of trial and error; what looks perfectly all right to the naked eye might look awful on screen. So always check the shot in the viewfinder – that's what it's there for.

The viewfinder or TV frames the shots that you get when you point the lens. So it is common to talk of framing shots, and of things being left of frame and right of frame. Note that the left or right of frame is left or right from the viewer's point of view. This can be confusing if, for example, you have someone giving a talk to camera. If you want them to move left of frame, you have to tell them to move to their right. If you want them to move right of frame, you have to tell them to move to their left.

Be aware of the background of the shot. A lot of movement in the background, assorted objects or bright colours, will all distract the viewer from what's happening in the foreground. If you can't change the angle, or do anything about the background, then try a tighter shot. To tighten a shot means to include more of the subject in the frame. This is done either by moving the camera closer to the subject, or by zooming in.

One effective way of getting rid of distracting backgrounds is to place the subject quite close to the lens. If the aperture is fairly wide, the background will be out of focus. This is because the wider the aperture, the narrower the depth of field – only a limited depth of view will be in focus.

When you are deciding what kind of shot to have, always think in terms of what the viewer will see and understand. Your choice of shots will affect how involved the viewer becomes.

HOW TO CHOOSE A SHOT

It will be important when writing scripts to describe shots correctly. There is a convention for describing shots, and most of the terms used have become part of the normal everyday language. Here are the main types of shot. The abbreviations are useful when scripting.

Long shot (LS)   A long shot of a person shows the whole of their body. It is often called a **wide angle shot (WA)**, which emphasises that the shot has a wide area in the frame. This shot is often used as an establishing shot at the beginning of a sequence to set the overall scene, so that the viewer can see, for example, how many people there are in a room, and where they are in relation to each other.

Medium Shot (MS)   This is a tighter shot, ie closer in, showing someone from waist up. It concentrates the viewer's attention on the person more than the surroundings.

Close-up (CU)   This is the shot to use for emphasis on what is being said, and to show emotions. It is also for showing detail.

Wide angle (W/A)   Medium shot (MS)   Close-up (CU).
or Long shot (LS)

These are the basic shots in television, film and video. All other shots are variations on these: **big close-up (BCU)**, **medium close-up (MCU)** and **medium long shot (MLS)**.

Big close-up (BCU)   Medium close-up (MCU)   Medium long shot (MLS)

You should apply the same shot terminology to objects as to people. However, you may have to be more specific when describing, for example, a medium shot of a car. There are a few other special names for certain types of shot which are less familiar. A shot with two people in the frame is called a **two-shot**, one with three in a **three-shot**, and with four or more, a **group-shot**.

2-shot   *3-shot*   *Group shot*

Interviews are often shot from behind the interviewer so that the viewer sees a part profile of the interviewer, but the interviewee (respondent) is shot almost head-on, full-face. This is a useful way of getting two people in shot when you want the viewer to concentrate on one person rather than the other. So this kind of shot is called an **over-the-shoulder (OSS) 2-shot**. It is usual to favour the respondent, since it is the answers which are more important than the questions!

This OSS favours the respondent standing on the right of frame.

Whenever you frame a shot, avoid getting the subject too close to the edge of the frame. When you play back the recorded picture on tape, some of the shot will be missing. TVs are 'overscanned'. This means they are set up at the factory so that some picture round the edge of the frame is lost. So when you frame shots in the viewfinder, you should always leave a 'safe area' around the edge of the frame, keeping the subject well away from the edge. Just as you have to do when taking a photograph, to allow for slight variations in printing.

The safe area is shaded. Get used to framing subjects away from the edge of the viewfinder.

HOW TO MOVE THE CAMCORDER OR CAMERA

The best guideline about moving is: don't – unless there's a good reason for it. Any movement which does not serve to help the action along will only make the viewer aware of your camerawork. And that's just what you don't want. You want their attention to be on what you are shooting, not on how it's being shot. The hallmark of good camerawork is that it shouldn't be noticed. Of course, you will hope that whoever sees your videos will be impressed by the camerawork, but that is a very different thing. No-one will be impressed by shaky shots and clumsy movement.

Even if you're using a tripod, it still takes a little practice before you can move around smoothly, especially with smaller and lighter equipment. The best technique is to stand right in to the camera, and use your own body to act as a counterbalance and support.

Pointing to the left and right whilst standing still is called **panning**. You will often need to use a pan to follow action. One of the best exercises to improve your control is to practise panning following people around. Some people find it easier to have the viewfinder a little away from the eye, rather than right up close. The reason for this is that when you are recording shots of people moving, unless it's a scripted and rehearsed sequence, you will not know exactly when they are going to move, or stop, or change direction. If you have your eye slightly away from the viewfinder, it is easier to anticipate what they're going to do next. However, the danger of this is that of taking the eye off the viewfinder. Keeping the eye right up close to the camera is better *if* you can keep the other eye open too.

Try and keep the subject slightly to the left of the centre line if you're panning right, and slightly to the right of it if you're panning left. This space in the direction the subject is looking is called

Looking room makes the shot seem more natural and makes life easier for the camera operator.

looking room. It not only makes the shot look more natural, it makes things very much easier for you as well.

The more space between the subject and the side of the frame they're moving toward, the less chance you'll lose them out of shot. Avoid following up a pan left with a pan right, and vice versa. It is very disorientating for the viewer.

You'll need to keep a little space above the subject's head too, between the top of their head and the top of the frame. This space is called **headroom**. Leave too much headroom, though, and the framing will no longer be natural. You should aim to keep the subject's eyes about one third of the way down the frame, whatever the size of shot.

Pointing up and down is called **tilting**. You would have to do this if, for example, you were making a sequence where someone was sitting in a chair, and then stood up. Even if you had framed this movement as a long shot, you would still have to tilt up slightly or the shot would look wrong. Remember where the subject's eyes should be, and you can't go far wrong.

Whatever the shot size, keep the subject's eyes roughly one third of the way down the frame and allow sufficient headroom.

When the camcorder or camera itself is moved, when following a subject down the street, for example, that is called a **tracking shot**. Tracking is quite difficult to do without practice, since both you and the subject are moving. It's quite hard to keep the subject in the same place in the frame with all that movement going on.

HOW TO HOLD THE CAMERA

Although camcorders and cameras are designed to be hand-held, keeping still is one of the first problems you will come up against.

It's not surprising if your first attempt at making videos is not 100% perfect; a lot of people find it difficult to take a holiday snap without acute camera shake. Even professional camera operators who work for broadcast television don't have to rely on keeping perfectly still when they're out shooting: they have a special body brace which acts as a counterweight to the heavier camcorders and cameras.

There are a number of things you can do to keep still. Perhaps the most important is to get yourself comfortable. Stand with your legs apart, and breathe in and out a few times to relax yourself before you press the trigger. If you can, lean up against a wall or a tree to give some support, or rest the camcorder or camera on the top of something, like a car, or even someone's shoulder.

Wear clothes that you feel comfortable in, and try not to get too hot. It takes up a lot of energy to keep still for long periods, especially when your arms are going to be above your waist – one hand holding the body of the camcorder or camera, the other adjusting the controls. If your camcorder or camera isn't one of those that can sit on the shoulder, then hold it in as close as you can to your body. Using one hand to operate the controls, support it firmly with the other arm.

If you are panning, turn the whole body, not just your arms. Try not to bob up and down when you pan. You'll find it helps not to move the feet during the pan if possible, but to keep them in the same position, spaced apart. It's possible to do this almost through a 360° pan.

To support the camera, hold it as close to the body as you can.

It is possible to pan in almost a full circle by keeping your legs apart and twisting the body.

HOW TO VARY THE SHOT

Using the zoom has many pitfalls. Common mistakes to try and avoid are zooming too fast, too jerkily, too often, and without cause. All camera movement should be slow and steady whenever possible. If you use the zoom to jerk the viewer suddenly into a close-up, and then yank them out to a long shot, and then in again, it all becomes a bit of a strain. The viewer won't be able to get involved in the video if you keep reminding him or her about your zoom lens!

You should use the zoom in a shot to draw the viewer's attention gradually to a particular part of the shot. The zoom itself should be so slow that it is not noticeable. This is hard to achieve using the electric zoom ... and not very easy using the manual zoom! Another use of the zoom is to pull out from a close-up to reveal more of the scene. You might use this where you want to bring someone else into the shot, or where the slow zoom out is used to heighten a dramatic effect, perhaps to add an element of surprise.

Avoid overusing the zoom effect – it soon becomes tiresome. Don't under-estimate how long the viewer needs to look at each shot in your video. You don't have to change the shot continually in order to make your videos interesting. It's better to choose your shot carefully in the first place, and then let the action taking place in the shot provide the necessary movement. If you are honest with yourself and self-critical, you will soon learn how long a particular shot needs to be. It isn't possible to generalise about that; it depends what shots have gone before, and how much action there is in the shot.

Once you zoom in to a subject, don't zoom out again. It won't look at all natural, and visually, it looks very messy. You should tremble before you zoom in; it is a very big step to take. Once in, stay in.

Avoid too many big close-ups; the effect will usually be too intrusive, unless you are dealing with highly charged, emotional and dramatic situations. Objects, on the other hand, can be highlighted very effectively using a range of all the shot sizes. And it is the close-up shots that make video such an ideal medium for presenting, demonstrating and illustrating such a wide variety of different topics and subject areas.

If you want to record a subject moving to the left or right *and* towards or away from the camera, you will have to pan, tilt and focus at the same time. That is no mean task, but it can be done. If it is a scripted sequence, then it is simply a matter of rehearsing until you learn your hand and finger positions throughout the shot.

If the sequence is unrehearsed, then it's not quite so easy. The secret is to make each movement very slowly indeed. Unless the subject is running very fast, you will not have to make any sudden camera movements or adjustment to focus. You are aiming to keep the subject in the same part of the frame, whether walking or running.

The subject is moving left to right. Keep him in the same position in the frame in each shot.

The more you can practise this, the easier you will find it to do. You need to be able to find the focus ring straightaway, and know which way to turn it for movement towards and away from the camera. Auto-focus is best avoided as its self-adjustment is rather too jerky to accomplish the gradual focussing that is necessary for this kind of shot.

If you are using auto-focus, it can give spurious and unwanted results. It should not, for example, be used when shooting through bars or railings, as it is generally the subject in the foreground which is selected for focus. It does not cope well with subjects walking or running, or with subjects not in the centre of the frame. These are deficiencies rather than faults as such, but they will still spoil your videos, so take care to select manual focussing whenever there is any doubt as to what the subject will do (which might well be most of the time!).

HOW TO BEGIN AND END SHOTS

It's a little clumsy to 'jump start' a video. One moment nothing, the next, something's happening. It takes a second or two for the viewer to realise what's going on, and by that time you've moved on to the next shot, and the viewer feels he or she might have missed something.

A better way is to record 20 seconds or so with the aperture closed. This is called 'black', although it'll appear far from black on the TV screen, more like grey. Then set up ready for the first shot – get the shot you want, focus, and so on. When all is ready, go to standby mode, and then, without moving the lens, carefully turn the iris ring to the closed position, marked 'c'. Start recording, and slowly fade up from black. This can be done electronically if you have an auto-fade switch. With others, you can get the same effect by doing a fade to black as before, and then switching to auto-iris once you have started recording. The third method is to fade up manually, but you have to make sure that you turn the iris smoothly without moving the camera itself, so losing the shot.

To fade up from black is an accepted way of starting a programme. It brings the viewer slowly into your opening shot, and prepares the way for what is to come. It is not a technique to use for every shot, though, or it would lose its impact, and be visually confusing.

It is equally acceptable to fade to black at the end of a programme. Some camcorders and cameras have an auto-fade out switch to achieve this effect; on others you will have to fade to black manually, again making sure that the iris ring is turned smoothly, and without losing the shot. If you have an auto-iris and no auto-fade out, you will have to switch to the manual setting before you can fade to black. If you can remember, change to manual iris before you start recording the final shot of your video. Auto-fade sometimes fades to white; and some cameras are switchable.

A similar effect to fading out a shot is to lose focus at the end of a shot by turning the focus ring until the shot is completely out of focus. This has to be done quite quickly, and the shot has to be really out of focus when you finish otherwise everyone will just think that your camerawork has got worse! The effect can also be used in reverse for opening a shot. However, use such trick effects sparingly, as in most cases they simply serve to make the viewer aware of camerawork, and that is precisely what you don't want to happen.

HOW TO USE AVAILABLE LIGHT

Most camcorders and cameras have an auto-iris facility which automatically adjusts the size of the aperture, according to the light level. Most cameras also have a separate iris control.

If you switch to manual iris, and open it too much in a brightly lit scene, the picture will take on a bleached look. You will lose contrast and details will become blurred and indistinct. On the other hand, if the aperture is not open enough, the picture will be dark, and it will be equally hard to make out details in the shot. The correct aperture setting is the right balance between the two. Use your judgement to decide this. It is much easier to do if you use a TV to monitor the shot, rather than the small electronic viewfinder. Most viewfinders, though, have a low light warning lamp which will glow if the scene is insufficiently lit.

Shooting in low light is unavoidable if you use your camcorder or camera regularly. Bad weather, large, poorly lit interiors, night work – these will all make heavy demands. You will have to use the widest aperture setting, which will be selected automatically if you switch to auto-iris.

Image-lag is a problem if you have a tube camera or tube camcorder. In low light the tube works less efficiently, and images are replaced more slowly, giving a ghosting effect. Most switch to a black and white type picture under *very* low lighting conditions. If there is one brighter part of a dimly lit shot, such as candles in a poorly lit church, you will get a streaking as the flame flickers, or as you pan across the light. And as we have already seen, focussing is more critical when you have to work in low light. Also, the lower the light you are working in, the harder it will be to focus.

A picture gain control, where fitted, increases the sensitivity of the camera to give clearer shots in low light. These work quite well, but will make the shot appear more grainy – rather like when a photograph is enlarged.

If you're working inside, any extra room lighting that you can use will give you a sharper picture. Fluorescent lights are particularly good, as are the domestic spot lights for increasing light in a small area. You could also use special extra lighting for video. However, in most cases, it is quite possible to get perfectly acceptable shots without special lighting.

The best lighting to use for video is daylight, which is the strongest light available. In fact bright sunlight is so strong that if you take your camera on holiday with you to the Mediterranean or other sunny climes, you will need a polarising filter to reduce the reflections caused by very bright sunlight. Remember that you can also use daylight when shooting indoors, using the light coming in through the window. You will need to use the daylight selection switch, if fitted.

Strong daylight, does, however, cause shadow problems. The auto-iris will self-adjust, and it usually averages the exposure for the shot. If you have positioned the subject so that the light is falling on one side of the face, for example, the unlit side will be much darker. The stronger the light, the darker the unlit side will be. One solution is to change position, moving the subject so that the light is falling evenly over the whole face. Another is to reduce the lighting level. If you're in sunlight, of course, this means finding somewhere out of direct sunlight. On a bright day, there will still be more than enough light to get a good picture.

A similar problem occurs when you try to shoot against a bright background. Try sitting someone in front of a window on a bright day. If you frame a long shot, their face will be just a silhouette. A medium shot will still give a dark face. Details and features will only be clearly visible if you frame a close-up or big close-up. These are the only shots where the face fills most of the frame, so excluding the bright background. If you try to get round this by switching to manual iris and opening the aperture to f 1.8, you'll just get a horrible bleached shot, and details still won't be clear. A backlight switch may compensate slightly, but it is better to avoid the problem in the first place.

TOP FIVE LIGHTING TIPS

Close-ups work better in low light than medium or long shots, where the details of the subject can easily become overshadowed – literally.

Set your white balance after you have decided on your camera position and what lighting you're going to use. Re-set whenever the light changes.

If you do a lot of work in sunlight or other bright lights, you will find it useful to have a reflector. These are available as accessories, and are made of a sheet of tough silver foil, which can be hand-held or mounted somewhere, such as on an adjacent wall. The idea is to reflect the available light onto the shaded side of a subject. Use a smooth one for a strong direct reflection, and a crumpled one for a diffuse reflection. Ordinary white card makes an effective improvised reflector; kitchen foil on one side will create a silver reflector.

Strong light from one source can cause shadow problems.
Use a reflector to fill out the shadows.

Never forget the damage that direct or reflected light can do to a tube. Always shut down the aperture and replace the lens cap before changing position, or making any adjustments to lighting.

Deal with any tube burns straightaway. Switch on the camera, and point the lens at an evenly lit wall until the burn disappears. If it remains after an hour, you'll need a new tube.

HOW TO GET THE BEST SOUND

The sound in your programmes is every bit as important as the pictures. It provides atmosphere and realism. Try turning the sound down and you'll realise how 'dead' a shot is without even background sound, or 'atmos' (atmosphere). For the best sound quality, you must use a separate microphone, rather than relying on a low quality built-in one. If you feel you can't manage to hold or set up a separate microphone, then fit one to the accessory shoe, if fitted, or tape it to the top of the camcorder or camera, insulating it from the body with felt or sponge. Even though the microphone position will be far from ideal, you will still get better results than if you use the built-in one.

The best place for a microphone is around 12 inches away from the subject, and pointing at a slight angle towards their mouth. Don't put it too close, or pointing directly at them, or you will pick up popping and hissing sounds as they speak. You can quite easily do some simple checks yourself by putting the microphone in different positions and making test recordings.

For presentations to camera, a table stand or floor stand will support the microphone and hold it at the correct angle for recording. If you are shooting interviews, your interviewer can hand-hold the microphone, turning it slightly to whoever is speaking. The more sensitive the microphone, however, the more careful you will have to be about moving it around during a shot.

Getting the sound roughly the same from shot to shot is a common problem. Most small-format VCRs and camcorders do not provide any electonic control over the level of sound recording. Audio AGC (automatic gain control) circuits will just give you a lot of background noise, and flatten out natural variations in sound frequencies and levels. You do, however, have control over the type of microphone that you choose. And you may have control over the kind of environment you record in, where the microphone is placed, and possibly the voice level of the speaker.

The place where you record will have a significant effect on the quality of your sound recording. In the open air the worst problem is caused by the wind. Even very slight breezes sound more like a gale when using an unprotected microphone. Even with a wind shield, strong winds will drown out voices. If you are hand-holding the microphone, you can reduce the effect of a strong wind by standing with your back to it, and so shielding the microphone with your body.

Another problem you will meet outside is the noise of traffic, roadworks, and the like. Here too, you can reduce the effect of these unwanted noises by positioning the microphone so that it is pointing away from the source of the noise.

Use your body to shield the microphone from the wind.

Point the microphone away from traffic noise.

For recording sound inside, you need to take special note of any echo. The more hard surfaces there are, the worse the echo will be. Echoes are caused by sound bouncing off of unabsorbent surfaces. So the more soft things there are around, such as carpets, curtains, soft furnishings and the like, the less sound will be reflected. This is why TV and sound studios often have acoustic tiles, which absorb sound very well, on the walls and ceilings. The sound characteristics of a room are called its acoustics.

Most table stands designed for stick microphones have rubber feet to absorb vibration, which is another sound hazard. You can protect the microphone from this even more by placing a piece of felt or similar soft material under the stand. But even a well-insulated table stand will pick up someone tapping their hands or feet against the table. Table stands are really only a compromise – better than resting the microphone on the table itself, but inferior to a floor stand.

A microphone can be securely held with a table stand

or a floor stand with a short boom.

The floor stand is adjustable for sitting or standing positions. The base is solid and heavy to support the upright and the cross piece. The cross piece is called the boom. It can be swung across a table, and its angle and length are easily adjusted by a locking screw on the upright.

Ideally, you should have an assistant to direct the microphone at whoever is speaking, monitoring the sound whilst recording is taking place, and keeping the microphone in the optimum position. Where this is not possible, you should aim to get as near to the right distance and angle as you can.

Does it matter if the microphone is in shot? Well, it depends on the type of video you are making. If you are making a drama, then a microphone in shot will be intrusive. You may want to consider a personal microphone, which can be hidden out of view under clothing. Each person speaking, though, will need their own microphone, so you will need to use a sound mixer. On the other hand, it is quite acceptable to have a microphone in shot for presentations, demonstrations, documentaries, and interviews.

There may be occasions when a microphone cable is inconvenient, such as where there are crowds, or where the microphone has to be some way from the camera or VCR. Here a radio microphone is a useful, if expensive, accessory.

BEFORE YOU GO OUT AND RECORD . . . .

You can get more out of the most basic video gear by adopting simple procedures and techniques. Be organised and methodical about checking equipment. Don't set up before you have done a reconnaissance ('recce') to find out the best positions for the camera and microphone. Be on the look-out for the best shot, and be alert enough to anticipate any unexpected movement. Avoid moving the camera unless there is a reason. Remember to frame shots in the safe area, and to leave looking room and headroom. Hold the camera as steady as you can, and avoid 'zoomitis'. It is effective to fade up and down at the beginning and end of a video. Monitor both pictures and sound before and during recording: lighting and sound play a major part in the quality of a programme.

Video Ideas
and Projects

Camcorders and cameras are the video equivalent of the instama-
tic camera. They are so simple to use that almost all you have to do
is point and shoot. Whereas video was once thought by many to be
suitable only for making elaborate programmes, now the video
snapshot has evolved.

Because the equipment is so compact and straightforward it can
be taken anywhere, battery-charged, ready for instant recording
of anything. It gives all the fun and interest of photography with
the added dimension of moving pictures and sound.

For this kind of *ad hoc* video, the smaller and lighter the equipment the better. So, like the smaller stills cameras, it's easy to take
the video equipment when out with family or friends, and ideal for
holidays. Video is also increasingly being used in industry and
commerce for less elaborate applications like the instant portrait
of the progress of a project, or reconnaissance of a new site.

There are no hard and fast rules for using video out and about –
you point and shoot what you want. Since the aim is simply to get
across the fun and atmosphere, rather than to communicate hard
information or ideas, your approach can be more relaxed.

However, to video most events – rallies, processions, royal
occasions, etc, you will get the atmosphere across better if you
video as an observer, rather than as a participant. If you video from
among a crowd, sound will be a confused mess, and the pictures
will be continually blocked by peoples' heads. Children will jump
up and down in shot, waving their hands and shouting 'Hello,
mum!' You will probably miss most of what's going on. If you can
video from a distance, you will be able to choose from a variety of
shots, and let the movement come from the event itself.

No matter how simple your subject is, you will be disappointed in
your results if you ignore too many of the techniques suggested in
this book. Nevertheless, even a video with a serious intention can be
fun to make, and creative and fresh in its content and approach.

HOW TO PLAN A VIDEO

Planning is the byword for good video. Equipment, subjects, locations, time – all these must be carefully planned to avoid failure

and disappointment. Everything that you shoot will be done better if you plan ahead. In particular, when you get an idea for a recording or programme, go through all the different possibilities before you decide on a particular approach. Think about what will work best visually, also getting as much human interest as you can. Remember that people will tell their own story better than you'll be able to tell it for them. Work out a shooting sequence, and keep to it unless there is good reason to change. If you do change it, make sure that your continuity is not affected.

When you know what you're going to record, go and visit some locations beforehand. Go, if you possibly can, on the same day and at the same time as you will be recording, so that you are aware of any possible disturbances. Don't for example visit on a Sunday if you're going to be recording on a Wednesday. If this can't be avoided, then of course any visit is better than none at all. Take note of where you might be able to charge batteries, where the toilets are, and if you're going to be there some time, what refreshments are available. If you haven't got your equipment with you, you can start to work out some camera angles in your mind, and take note of any particular sound or lighting problems. Write these details down in a production notebook.

You might need permission to shoot on private property. This is not necessary if you're in the street or other public place, unless you are likely to be causing any sort of obstruction or disturbance. If that is likely, then it would be as well to advise the police in advance. The Metropolitan Police issue an information sheet to professional video and film crews, who are more likely to fall foul of the law because of the crowds they tend to attract (see p. 66).

In spite of this, don't be afraid to record spontaneously. The more you plan the various recordings that you make, the more you will find yourself being able to cope with the unexpected. Part of the art of good camerawork and direction is being able to improvise where necessary, and to work out quickly what the best shots are.

Allow yourself plenty of time for whatever recording you are doing. The time it takes you to set up and check that everything's working will vary depending on how complex the programme is, and to some extent on the sort of equipment you've got. When you're planning time, allow for travelling, rigging, checking, rehearsing, recording, de-rigging, and travel back. Estimate how long each will take, and then add half as much again as a contingency for things going wrong. As a rough guide, the more control you want over the recording, the longer it will take to set up and to record.

METROPOLITAN POLICE

FILMING IN STREETS

The following notes are issued for the information and guidance of persons undertaking filming in the streets and public places:-

(1) Nothing in the nature of a staged crime or street disturbance will be permitted.

(2) No filming can be permitted which would interfere with the operation of the parking meter schemes or give rise to any contravention of Road Traffic Acts or Regulations.

(3) Any filming must be undertaken on the sole responsibility of the promoters and participants, and no facilities can be granted by Police.

(4) The Commissioner of Police has no power to authorise the use of streets for the purposes of filming and does not issue permits purporting to do so, but police will not normally object to proposed filming provided that:-

    (a) No obstruction or annoyance is caused and the directions of police on duty are observed.

    (b) In the event of complaints being made or annoyance being caused filming ceases immediately at the request of Police.

    (c) Where artificial lighting is used care is taken to ensure that no obstruction or danger is caused by cables, wires, etc., and no danger or annoyance is caused by dazzle from the lights.

    (d) As far as possible filming is arranged to take place when traffic, both vehicular and pedestrian, is lightest, e.g., on a Sunday morning.

    (e) When it is proposed to film actors dressed in police uniforms, rehearsals are to be carried out in plain clothes. The fitting of gongs, bells, two-tone horns and blue flashing lights to pseudo-police vehicles is prohibited by law.

    (f) Any special requirements of police about a particular filming are observed.

Copies of this information leaflet (MP72 E)
are obtainable from Scotland Yard's 'B' Department.

HOW TO TELL A STORY

A story is basic to a video. Without a story, a series of shots have no relation to one another, and the viewer may soon lose interest in the video, especially if it is rather long. It is very easy to develop a story with video. All it needs is a little thought *before* you start shooting.

For example, let's suppose you are making a video of a boy, Matthew, playing with a dog, Charlie, in the garden. You want to show it to some of the family who live some way away, or play it during the winter to remind you of summer, or to keep it for when Matthew grows up. You could just take a number of different shots, close-ups, medium shots, and long shots, just as you would if you were taking snapshots. Although this would provide snapshots with movement, you could do more.

The secret of telling any sort of story to people is to keep them guessing, not to show everything at once. So in the video of Matthew and the dog, continual wide angle shots wouldn't really keep our interest. Nor would a number of different unrelated close-ups – that would just be confusing. A jumbled mixture of different types of shot would suggest a story that wasn't really there, so that would be confusing too.

The best way to show Matthew and the dog is to work out a simple story line – just half a dozen shots or so – each shot moving the story along a little at a time. For example:

Shot 1
– MS Charlie;

Shot 2
– CU Stick;

Shot 3
– W/A Charlie sitting;

Shot 4
– W/A Matthew picking up stick;

Shot 5
– CU Charlie's tail wagging;

Shot 6
– W/A Charlie chasing stick;

Shot 7

– CU Matthew praising and stroking Charlie.

You stop recording at the end of each shot, and frame up the next shot. This takes a bit more effort than doing a continual recording, but the result will look better, and it will be more interesting. Notice the variety of shots to use: close-ups for detail, medium shots to show the surroundings and the action taking place, and the wide-angle to show the whole scene. Making different shots appear as a continuous sequence in this way is confusingly known as 'editing in the camera'. This is the simplest way to make a video. The 'editing' in this case is in fact simply the selecting of certain shots rather than others to record.

If Matthew is playing this game with Charlie over and over again, you won't even have to interrupt the game to set up each shot. The viewer won't know if, for example shot 2 is recorded the first time the stick is thrown, and shot 6 the tenth time. You could set each shot up specially, but it probably wouldn't be as spontaneous.

It's not necessary, or even a good thing, to show all of the action. For example, between shot 2, the stick, and shot 4, Matthew picking it up, there is a shot of Charlie, shot 3. We are seeing Charlie's reaction. You don't then have to show Matthew walking over to the stick. The viewer will accept that you have compressed time, and the three shots will seem perfectly logical and correct. You will have kept visual continuity. The technique is used continually in television and film, and you too can make use of it to suggest a lot of things occurring without your videos lasting for hours.

Using different shots to tell a story gives a different angle and view on the subject. And by placing one shot next to the other, you are inviting the viewer to make a link between them. Because you show Matthew picking up the stick, followed by Charlie's tail wagging, you are suggesting a link between them: that Charlie is excited at the prospect of chasing the stick. This is why video is creative – by using visual images, people can be influenced to your point of view. It also accounts for why video has often been seen as a powerful, persuasive medium – hence its widespread use by individuals and groups with ideas and opinions to get across.

For sound in the video about Charlie and Matthew, all that is needed is the background sound which occurs. A commentary would be unnecessary, and would spoil the natural atmosphere.

You will probably find that once you start using video creatively, you will begin to pay special attention to the techniques used in televised plays, films and documentaries.

Try to notice particularly how shots are put together, and how restrained camera movements are. Commentary or dialogue is often kept to a minimum, to allow the visual effect and the atmosphere to speak for itself. You can put all these techniques to use yourself in your recordings.

TAKING VIDEO ON HOLIDAY

For more and more people, video is replacing the stills camera to take on holiday. The camcorder, particularly, is designed as a go-anywhere, record-anywhere machine. You could either take it in the custom made bag or case, or in a beach bag, protected from sand and dirt by a plastic bag.

Make sure you protect it from sun, sand and sea. If the equipment gets too hot, the cassette housing could warp, and you may have to replace it if the tape cassettes no longer fit. Sand and seawater will both do a lot of damage if they get inside the VCR. Some camcorders have a waterproof protective shell available as an accessory, but without one of these, you must take great care in keeping out the elements.

For holiday recordings, it is useful, though by no means essential, to have the place and date on the recording. To have this information for a few seconds at the beginning of the recording will be helpful in years to come. You can do this if you have electronic titling with date superimposition. However it's quite straightforward simply to make up a caption with the date and place on it, and record it at home before you leave; you'll then have a record of where and when all the subsequent shots were taken.

You will find your recordings more interesting when you play them back if you involve people, rather than just scenery. If you are with your family, then record them enjoying themselves. That way, you can also get the atmosphere of the place, but at the same time make the video personal to you and the rest of your family. The same applies if you holiday with friends. You could even try interviewing the landlady!

If you go to visit an interesting place, your video will be more lively if you can find out some information beforehand, and add a voice-over commentary to the shots you take.

Try to keep sequences short and varied. Use a mixture of shots, and try to think what *you* would look for as a visitor to a place. You can make use of signs and signposts as ready made captions to help the viewers know where they are. Aim to work out a sequence of shots that will develop the story of your visit.

If you're visiting, say, an historic house, start with wide angle shots of the grounds and exterior, then some medium shots, then go to close-ups of detail. Record a sequence showing the entrance, and that will serve as your link to record inside. Avoid shooting out of the window now, or you will disorientate the viewer. Stay inside and record a series of medium shots followed by close-ups to show detail. If you're tracking and the house is poorly lit, watch your focus, as the depth of field will be minimal. In poorer light, it's often better to set up a series of still shots, where you have more control over the camera angle, and focus can be set more accurately than if you're moving around.

If you are around the sea, a lake or a river, glare and reflection from water can make it impossible to make out any detail of things happening on or in the water. It is useful in these situations if you have a polarising filter. This will cut down glare, and give a clearer shot. Remember, though, not to use auto-focus when shooting scenes involving water. The same problem, and the same solution, applies to shooting through glass.

Activity holidays are particularly suitable subjects for video. These kinds of holiday are now available covering all sorts of interests as wide ranging as wine tasting, cycling, drama and computing. As long as you are fairly unobtrusive, most organisers and participants will have no objection to you making a video featuring what's going on. It might even be positively welcomed if the holiday involves acquiring some skill that could be recorded and played back as a teaching and learning aid.

Don't forget to take plenty of battery power with you, and an RF lead if there's a TV set available to play back on while you're there. Although you probably want the video primarily as a record for years to come, it's also fun to be able to play back at the end of the day. Note that if you go overseas, you will have to take a UK TV set or monitor with you to play back whilst on holiday! Some foreign TV standards are not compatible with those in the UK.

HOW TO MAKE A PROGRAMME ABOUT A HOBBY

Almost every hobby can be the subject of an interesting video. As a general guideline, you need to include individuals talking about their hobby. This can be done straight to camera, or as a presentation with props etc, or as a voice-over commentary to appropriate shots of the hobby in progress. The last one will probably be the most realistic, manageable and interesting format for most hobbyists who may not turn out to be accomplished presenters. You need to keep away from too much on the general aspects of the hobby, as that could soon become rather dull. You can't assume that the viewer is necessarily going to be interested in the hobby itself. Concentrate instead on the unusual aspects. Keep a look out for what is different or surprising. You are going to have to capture the viewer's imagination, so your job is to try to make a hobby, which in itself may not actually seem interesting to you, appear to be so. This will test your skill as a programme-maker to the full.

Let's look at train spotting as an example. This may seem, on first sight, the dullest of hobbies. But think of the visual potential. The age of steam may have passed, but shots of diesel trains pulling in and out of stations can still be impressive. Concentrate on the unusual, so for example rather than asking how many different types of diesel trains there are, ask about the hardest trains to spot, and about why the train spotter spots.

The viewer will learn more about train spotting if you can reveal the character of the train spotter and what motivates him or her, rather than a list of assorted facts about trains. Combine that with the atmosphere of the trackside, and you have the makings of an excellent programme. If you need to get access to railway property to make your programme, then you need official approval first. Contact the station manager, explaining exactly what you'd like to do. Permission is not usually withheld.

HOW TO RECORD CHILDREN GROWING UP

Children are a good subject for video, as they are usually quite un-selfconscious in front of the camera. Increasingly, the family video album is taking its place alongside the family photo album. Usually it is major events that are chosen for recording children, such as birthday parties, sports days and Christmas. But a video of normal everyday situations can be made just as interesting. In fact as a record of the child's nature and personality, it will give a more typical picture.

The recordings can be done in a systematic way, or spontaneously. Either way, make sure that the date is recorded on tape so that the record is complete. If you can't superimpose the date

71

electronically, then it's easy to make a simple caption by writing or typing the date on paper, and recording it using the macro setting on the zoom lens.

A simple date caption handwritten in felt-tip pen.

It's best to be as unobtrusive as you can, to try to catch the children off guard. Don't forget to include their friends, toys, and any pets as well, as you are aiming for as complete a picture of them at that age as possible. As children tend to shout a lot when they're playing together, getting enough sound isn't usually too much of a problem!

A good way to make an unobtrusive recording is to set up the equipment, switch on and record a wide angle shot. Then move away as if getting ready, but have the camera still recording. Everyone will carry on, thinking you haven't started.

If you want an archive of your children growing up, it will be useful to have an index of what's on the tape. If you use the digital counter numbers, it will be an easy matter to find particular sequences when required. If you change equipment, though, you may have to index the material again, as the new counter may run at a different speed. If you buy a different format, make sure you copy the tapes onto the new format.

HOW TO VIDEO A LIVE BAND

Video is frequently being used with music. Images and sound complement each other well, and hardly a pop record is produced now without a video to accompany it. We'll be looking at how to produce a pop video later, but it is also possible to make a straightforward unedited recording of a band.

The approach to recording music has to be rather different from other types of recording. Music has its own built in sequence, and if you disturb that by cutting and recording only parts of a song, you will ruin the music, and the recording won't make sense. You have to make a continuous recording of the whole of each number.

Sound can be recorded either through a microphone, or direct from an output of the band's amplifier. If you use the amplifier method, you will, however, lose all ambient sound; you'll only get the music. This won't convey the atmosphere of the performance, as there won't be any crowd reaction, but the sound quality of the music itself will certainly be better than if you use a microphone. If you have a separate microphone, direct it at one of the loud-speakers so that it picks up a minimum of reflected sound. Be careful not to hold it too close, particularly if it's a loud band, or you'll overload the audio circuits, and the sound will be very dis-torted. However you record sound, monitor the level carefully using headphones. If you're using a separate microphone, and you've got no audio level control, move away if it sounds distorted. Record some quieter numbers to get the best idea of the quality of the band's music.

For visuals, don't just keep to a wide angle shot. If you know the music well, and you know when the instrumental solos are going to come, you can pan from soloist to soloist as they are featured. Close-ups of instruments, hands, and facial expressions will all help to convey the atmosphere. Turn the camera round to the audience as well, not only at the end of numbers, but during them too. It will reflect well on the band to see the audience enjoy them-selves. Other interesting camera positions are behind the band, shooting through them with the audience in the background, and at the side to get another variation of angle. By all means try out some 'Top of the Pops' type effects such as fast zooming in time to the music, but unless you have a CCD or MOS imager, don't point at spotlights. Be wary of reflections of lights on guitars and drums too, as they often have highly reflective chrome fittings.

HOW TO VIDEO A WEDDING

A video is now as much a part of most wedding ceremonies as the wedding photos. A professional wedding video often demands proper editing, but weddings are also ideal occasions for anyone to capture the atmosphere and excitement of the occasion. There is always plenty of colour at weddings, with everybody dressed up and lots of flowers around. Video is good for highlighting the happiness of the occasion.

The formal groups that the photographer will gather together for the photos before and after the ceremony are useful to video as a record of who was there, but you should concentrate mainly on the informal groupings. The most enjoyable moments will be those where you manage to get people off guard, the candid shots when they are seeing people they might not have seen for years, and standing chatting in informal groups.

Some of the most interesting shots can be recorded before the ceremony itself, showing the bride and bridesmaids getting ready, and the arrival of the wedding car. However, you can't record everything. Aim to capture the flavour of the occasion and, above all, concentrate on action and movement.

It is often possible to record inside the church, but it is essential to ask the vicar's permission first. You must, of course, be unobtrusive, and it is worth asking the vicar about the best shooting position. Once you have chosen your spot, as a courtesy to all concerned it is important to stay there and not move around during the ceremony.

Sound can be rather booming where there are hard stone walls and high roofs, but for a general impression it should be adequate.

Of course, video is ideal for recording the speeches. If you can use a tripod, and set up a separate microphone – perhaps hand-held by an assistant – then you will have an impressive and unique record which cannot be captured by photos alone.

Recording the wedding speeches,
with an assistant holding the microphone.

Whether or not you can record the reception effectively may depend on how good the lighting is. You may well be asked at the reception to play your recording of the ceremony back for everyone to see! Obviously when you video a wedding, if you make a mistake it's irrevocable, so be doubly meticulous about your checklist and procedure.

If you video weddings regularly, you will, no doubt, develop your own style. Careful use of titles, captions and music can all enhance a wedding video.

It is a good idea to liaise with the official photographer. Your paths will cross many times, so the relationship might as well be amicable! Some photographers themselves now provide a video service, others might be willing to work in partnership with you.

HOW TO USE VIDEO FOR CCTV

CCTV, or closed circuit television, is the name given to the use of video to relay sound and pictures to an audience. It is closed, because the relay is not broadcast, but connected to TVs or monitors by fixed leads. Typical applications for this are meetings, lectures and demonstrations where there is a larger audience than can fit into the room, hall or lecture theatre. The shots may or may not actually be recorded onto videotape.

This use of video is invaluable where the subject is not normally visible from a distance. An example might be a cookery demonstration to a large number of people, or a physics experiment, perhaps. The pictures can be relayed to a large screen or to a number of smaller screens. These can be set up in the same room as the demonstration, or in one or more adjacent rooms. If a tripod is used, it's possible to do without an operator, once a suitable shot has been framed. The shot needs to be wide enough so that it will contain any movement that might take place in any direction. For detailed demonstrations it would be necessary to operate by hand, or by remote control. Pan, tilt, focus and zoom can all be operated by wired remote control. The camera is fixed to a mounting which is connected by cable to a remote control panel. A special camera is required that is capable of being driven in this way.

Many theatres now use CCTV to relay the performance to the foyer, so that latecomers don't miss any more of the show once they arrive, and also so that ushers can see the most appropriate time to show people to their seats. The camera is usually fixed to a bracket on the ceiling or wall, taking a wide angle shot of the whole stage area.

HOW TO ANALYSE SPORTING ACTION WITH VIDEO

Video is widely used in sports analysis – to examine tennis strokes, football set pieces, triple jump technique, weight lifting balance and timing, and so on. It can be used as a coaching aid, or by the players themselves to practise and analyse particular movements or strokes. In almost every sport, all the top teams have invested in video as a way of improving performance.

The key advantage of video in sports analysis is that it gives the individual a chance to see himself or herself *in situ*: to see the mistakes which may well not be apparent when on the field of play. It also allows the participant to compare his or her performance directly with that of others. With correct coaching, errors can be highlighted, and strategies devised to correct them. Subsequent efforts can similarly be recorded for analysis.

*A camcorder is used by many football clubs
and other teams to analyse tactics.*

The facility to play back as many times as required, to play in slow motion, and to freeze frame are all valuable for sports analysis. In certain circumstances, for example if you needed to show that a football player was not covering a large enough area, it would be useful to have fast forward search, which would highlight patterns of movement.

Sport comes over very well on video; not surprisingly, it is one of the most popular televised activities. Even with one camera, it is possible with a zoom lens to record both team and individual effort. Usually a higher than usual camera position is advisable so that movement can be more readily identified. A standard 6 × 1 zoom lens will often give quite sufficient magnification, but you may find you need a more powerful lens.

HOW TO KEEP IN TOUCH BY VIDEO

The message tape, or video letter, is a novel way of keeping in touch with distant friends and relatives. All that is required is for you and the recipient to have a VCR. You connect your camera, fix it to the tripod, and record you and your family's news and greetings. Then it needs to be packed in a good stout envelope before posting to its destination.

You need to check that the recipient has the same video format as you; if not, then either you, or they, will need to get a copy made onto the right format. If the tape is going overseas, you need to check the colour standard system in operation for TV in that country. If it's different, you or the recipient may have to get a standards conversion of the tape.

One idea if you both have video is to use the same tape for messages back and forth, taking care, of course, not to over-record previous recordings. In this way you build up a unique memento on one tape without the need to edit.

If the tape is going overseas, then it's a good idea to include a range of information in it: the sort of things that are usually taken for granted, such as a typical shopping basket, newspaper extracts, shots of your house, street and car, the neighbours saying hello, and so on. You could do the same sort of thing for your grandchildren to see; imagine if video was around 50 years ago, before the second world war, or a hundred years ago in the Victorian era!

There are many media groups throughout the country who give help, advice and training. They are often well equipped with amateur and semi-professional equipment which they either loan or hire. You can meet other people who are interested in making videos who may help you or might appreciate your help. Either contact your local Regional Arts Association or write to The Media Centre, South Hill Park, Bracknell, Berkshire RG12 4PA.

PART TWO
■

Further Steps

Adding Equipment and Accessories

BEFORE YOU READ ON

Making your own videos should be simple and straightforward. The equipment is widely available, and there are many basic, easy to operate versions, which will deliver good pictures and sound. A lot of people, though, are not happy with their results. One or two trys and the equipment gets put away and forgotten about. If you're one of those people, don't despair. Use 'Part One: Getting Started' to improve your technique, a little at a time. 'Part Two: Further Steps' is for those who are looking for more challenges. In it, there's more on equipment, more on techniques, and more applications. 'Further Steps' starts with editing. Editing opens up lots of possibilities for making more polished videos simply by using your own VCR and borrowing someone else's. But don't neglect your camera work and audio recording. Good pictures and sound are the cornerstones of any video, no matter how advanced you and your equipment become.

HOW TO CONNECT TWO VIDEOS FOR COPYING AND EDITING

You can copy and edit tapes between any video format. All that is needed is a VCR or camcorder that will play the original tapes, which is called the Play VCR, and a VCR to record the copies or edited programmes, called the Record or Edit VCR.

When you shoot with video, it is called a first generation recording. When a copy or edited version is made, that is second generation (one transfer has taken place to another tape). If you shoot a video, edit it, and then make a copy, the copy is third generation.

Some picture quality is lost during each transfer. Sound quality is also slightly reduced. Quality has to be kept high during the original shoot and the editing if a third generation tape is to be watchable.

For copying, it helps to have a TV or monitor to check what is being copied. It is connected to the Record VCR, but it will replay sound and pictures from the Play VCR.

It is vital to have a TV or monitor for editing, where you will be copying some shots and not others. To check visual continuity when editing, it is even better to have two, one for each VCR. Then you can see the Edit In and Edit Out points clearly on the two screens, and assess whether the visual link will be satisfactory.

To copy or edit, use the audio and video connectors at the back of the VCR. These carry pure audio and video, which will give better quality than using the antenna (or RF) connection.

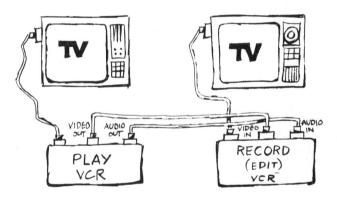

How to connect VCRs and TVs for copying and editing.

Switch everything on. Put the original recording in the Play VCR and a blank in the Record VCR. You can re-use an old tape for copying or editing onto, but the plastic 'erase protect' tab at the back of the cassette has to be intact. If it isn't, you can tape over it with masking tape and fool the VCR.

Switch off the tuner-timer to copy tapes. Cue the Play VCR at the beginning of the sequence you want to copy or edit. Use Rewind if there's a lot of tape to rewind, then Play and Search to cue the tape 10 seconds before the start of the sequence you want.

Cue up the blank tape in the Record VCR where you want the copy to start.

Set the Play VCR to Play/Pause, and the Record VCR to Record/ Play/Pause. Release Pause on the Play VCR, and watch the picture on the screen. At exactly where you want the copy or edit to start, release Pause on the Record VCR. The copy is now being recorded.

If you are editing, use Pause again on the Record VCR at the exact point you want the next sequence to begin. Find the next sequence on the Play VCR quickly, and copy that in the same way. You have to work fast, because most VCRs will go to Stop after a few minutes in Pause mode.

Once the copy is made, play it through, checking particularly for picture roll at the editing points. If there are rolls, you have the choice of leaving them in, or starting again from the last roll-free edit. Label the copy with title, date of recording and length. Remove the plastic tab or sticky tape to prevent it being recorded over accidentally.

WHAT CONNECTORS AND LEADS YOU NEED

For pure video to video signals, ask for 75 Ohm co-axial cable. This shields the TV signal from other radio frequency transmissions, such as couriers and CB radio. The cable consists of a centre copper wire, which is encased in plastic. This in turn is covered in a copper braid. This then has a final plastic covering. The distance between the centre and outside wires should be kept the same along the cable run, so avoid bending or tight coiling of the cable. The longer the cable, the weaker the signal, so to avoid signal loss, keep cables as short as possible.

The most common video connector is the BNC, which uses a bayonet fitting.

A BNC video connector.   *A phono audio connector.*

Audio connections should only be made with good quality

screened audio cable. This consists of two plastic-covered wires, and a copper braided wire, all in a plastic casing. The most common audio connector is the phono.

Adaptors are widely available for adapting one type of connector to fit another, although it is better to have the correct leads made up if you are using an adaptor regularly, as the connection will be more secure.

It is possible to copy pictures and sound from VCR to VCR using a single antenna lead. You have to tune the Record VCR to the test signal of the Play VCR in this case. But modulating the video signal to radio frequency and then demodulating results in a loss in quality which is very noticeable on copies.

The lead is connected from RF Out on the Play VCR to RF In on the Record VCR. Use standard 75 ohm co-axial cable. The connector, which may be male or female, is usually called a co-axial connector (or co-ax) or antenna connector. A simple adaptor will convert a male co-ax to female, and vice-versa.

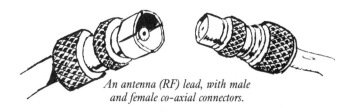

An antenna (RF) lead, with male and female co-axial connectors.

More than one copy can be made at a time by connecting VCRs in a chain via A/V In and Out sockets. A similar procedure is possible using the RF In and Out sockets and antenna leads.

VIDEO LIGHTING EQUIPMENT

You may, at times, be forced into using extra lighting if you want to record somewhere which is very dark, or if you want to record outside at night. Or you may need the higher quality picture that extra lighting will give, such as if you want to edit a programme, and then make further copies for people. You may need to increase the depth of field of a shot, or the subject of lighting itself might interest you, and you may want to try out different lighting effects, and use lights creatively to add atmosphere and impact to your video recordings.

The most straightforward type of extra lighting to use is ordinary domestic lighting. By switching on more lights, and, if possible, directing them at the shooting area, you can make some improvements to the lighting level. Spotlights which can be angled as required are the easiest to use, as the light can be confined to a small area.

When adding extra lighting, take care to avoid pools of light. You should aim for an even increase in light over the whole area in shot. Table lamps, for example, might appear to light a room, but on video only parts will be lit while other parts will appear darker. For a more intense light, you could use photo floods – high intensity filament lamps which are really designed for photographic use. These do, however, burn out very quickly; they will only last a few hours if used continually. This makes them rather unsuitable for video use. They are quite cheap though, and you may be able to pick some up second-hand through the photographic press.

The best high-intensity artificial lighting to use with video is the tungsten-halogen lamp. They are available in a variety of wattages, depending on the area you need to light. The most common are 800W or 1000W (1KW), three or four of which would light a part of a room, an interview, or other reasonably confined project. Tungsten-halogen lamps have a colour temperature of 3200 to 3400 °K which is the colour temperature at which video cameras are designed to work best. The lamps are adjustable to give a bright spot of light or a softer flood of light.

It is because different types of light vary in their colour temperature that you have to adjust the white balance of a video camera. The higher the colour temperature, the bluer the light actually is; the lower the colour temperature the redder the light is. So daylight is much bluer than tungsten-halogen light, as its colour temperature is roughly twice as great. You can see the effect of this for yourself if you adjust the white balance of your camera inside in artificial light, and then shoot outside without re-setting the white balance. The shots recorded outside will have a bluish cast to them.

The colour temperature of ordinary domestic light bulbs is about 2800°K, and of fluorescent daylight tubes about 4800°K. The colour temperature of photofloods is the same as that of tungsten-halogen lamps. So it's important to adjust white balance whenever you vary the type of lighting you use.

Tungsten-halogen lamps can be bought singly, or in kits of four with a carrying case. As well as the lamp itself, you will need tripods or clips to support the lamps, and scrims. These are metal gauze diffusers which are clipped to the front of the lamp as required, and used to soften the light output whilst not altering its colour temperature. The lamps are also supplied with 'barn doors', which are adjustable metal shades, which are used to restrict where the light falls. They make it easier to control shadows and define more clearly the contribution of each lamp to the total lighting effect.

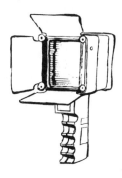

A hand-held tungsten-halogen video lamp.

Some smaller sizes of tunsten-halogen lamp can be battery operated. Kits are available consisting of one or more lamps with a battery belt or pack, and a connecting lead, all fitted in a rugged aluminium case. Some have handles for hand holding, whilst others have camera brackets for mounting on the accessory shoe on top of the camera, or butterfly clips for attaching to stands, girders, etc.

These lamps are quite suitable for night-time exterior location work. One would also be a useful spare or addition to a set of mains-powered lights. The battery packs and belts used to power portable lamps are the same as those you would use to replace the internal VCR battery. So a portable kit would give you the option of increased recording and playback time on location. The power belts and packs have built in charging units, and can be recharged by plugging direct into the mains. Some can also be topped up on location during breaks in shooting via a cigar lighter socket in a car.

All tungsten-halogen bulbs are coated with a chemical which is quite sensitive to grease. You should therefore avoid touching the bulbs with your fingers, but replace them using the card protective cover with which they are supplied. The bulbs also get very hot in use, and take about 5 minutes to cool down. It is better not to move the lamps during this time, as the bulbs are more easily damaged when they are hot.

A portable battery-operated lighting kit.

A tungsten-halogen bulb.

For safety reasons, when using the lamps with tripods, make sure that the base is firm and secure. Splay the three legs to their maximum extent, and use a mains extension lead with each one, so that the short lead is not pulling away from the lamp, possibly causing it to topple over. Check the current rating of the lamps you use. The most common each draw about 3⅓ amps, so you can safely run three from one 13 amp power socket if necessary.

The tripods extend to about 8 to 10 feet high, which provides a good lighting angle. Unfortunately, though, the higher the lamp is positioned, the more unstable it will be, as the centre of gravity will be further from the ground. If you can get hold of some sandbags, a couple of those holding the base down are an excellent safety precaution.

If the lighting outside is not strong enough, you can add a lamp, provided you raise its colour temperature by mounting a blue gel in front of it. Take care over colour balance, or the picture will have an uneven colouring. Other coloured gels are also available to create different coloured effects on a background.

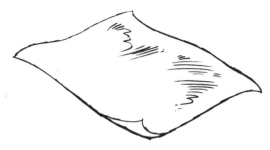

A blue lighting gel can be used to raise the colour temperature of a tungsten-halogen lamp to daylight level.

WHAT EXTRA LENSES CAN BE USED WITH VIDEO?

Apart from the standard zoom lens supplied with your video camera, extra lenses can broaden the scope of your programme making. The most useful is a wide angle lens. This is a fixed focal length lens, ie no zoom. The standard zoom lens must be unscrewed, and replaced by the new lens. Lenses used for stills photography can be held in place in front of a camcorder or camera lens by hand, or jammed into the lens hood. The wide angle lens is useful in small areas where the angle of acceptance of the zoom lens is too narrow to allow a wide angle shot. You have to take care not to use a lens which gives too wide an angle, however, as the picture will look distorted. The extreme example is called a fisheye lens, and that will give a curved panorama all around the camera.

There is a choice of zoom lenses available, from the standard 6 × 1 up to 14 × 1. The higher magnification is excellent for occasions when you do not want to get too close to the subject, for example in recording wildlife. It becomes even more important that the camera is tripod mounted when higher magnification zoom lenses are used, as any slight camera shake is also magnified.

CHOOSING THE BEST MICROPHONE FOR THE JOB

There is a wide range of microphones available which are suitable for use with video. You should choose your microphone carefully, as various types have different sound patterns.

Those which accept sound in a broad area from the direction in which they are pointed are called **directional**, or sometimes

uni-directional. These are also sometimes called **cardiod microphones,** which refers to their heart-shaped sound pattern.

Directional or cardioid microphone.

Directional microphones which are highly directional are called **gun microphones**. These are often used on location when the microphone has to be out of shot, because they are very effective in cutting out sound outside their very narrow sound pattern.

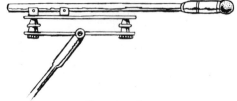

Gun microphone.

Hand microphones can never be held perfectly still, so need to accept sound from a broader area than directional microphones. They are thus omni-directional. They have a better frequency response than directional microphones, and pick up less wind, breath and mechanical noise; they also perform more evenly when the speaker varies his or her distance from the microphone.

Hand-held (omni-directional) microphone.

Personal microphones, which are either clipped to clothing, or taped to the body, are omni-directional, but only within a relatively confined area. These are ideal for use on the move, or where the microphone has to be concealed.

Personal microphone.

Radio microphones make use of a radio transmitter and receiver to feed signals to the VCR. Because they are classed as radio transmitters, they require a licence to use. (Contact the Department of Industry (radio regulatory): 01–275 3058.) Virtually any sort of microphone can be used, but it is generally the personal microphone which is worn when wireless operation is needed. The subject must wear, or have taped to his or her body, a small battery-powered radio transmitter, which the microphone is wired up to. A receiver tuned to the same frequency as the transmitter, picks up the sound signals and transmits them to the VTR via its microphone socket. However, because the transmission is quite low powered, obstructions such as buildings and cars frequently interfere with the signal.

For commentary work, when there is a lot of background noise, a **lip ribbon microphone** is ideal. This is designed to be held right in front of the mouth. The correct distance between the microphone and the mouth is critical, and is achieved by placing the top lip against the upper guard when it is in use. You can see examples of this type of microphone at some televised sports events.

Lip ribbon microphone.

Pressure zone microphones are designed to be used where sound needs to be picked up over a larger area. They are placed on a smooth solid surface, and because they pick up only reflected sound, they work well where the acoustics are poor.

Pressure zone microphone.

When you're choosing a microphone, remember that the reason for using a separate microphone, rather than the built-in one, is to get better quality. Microphones are sensitive and highly sophisticated pieces of equipment, and need to be well made to reproduce faithfully the human voice range. Therefore go for the best that you can afford.

The output of a battery-operated condenser microphone is greater than that of a dynamic one, although the latter is more sensitive to wind noise. On the other hand, dynamic microphones tend to be more robust, and there are no batteries to run down.

Some higher quality microphones can be powered from a sound mixer, or from a separate battery pack. This is called phantom power, and combines the advantages of improved frequency response and no batteries.

The impedance, or AC electrical resistance, of the microphone must roughly match that of the VCR. VCRs may have low or high impedance microphone inputs, and some may be borderline, so this must be checked out carefully. 600 ohms (low impedance) is common. The necessary information may be in the instruction book; if not contact the manufacturer.

WHY YOU MIGHT NEED A SIMPLE SOUND MIXER

The majority of small format VCRs have only one microphone socket. If you want to use two or more microphones for your video recordings, you will need to use a sound mixer. Most small sound mixers are battery operated, and accept up to four microphones. These are mixed together to one or two outputs, which you feed into the Audio In socket(s) of your VCR.

The audio level of each input can be set independently, using slider or rotary controls. It is important to set each microphone level carefully for maximum level without distortion, particularly if the programme is to be edited.

Headphones can be plugged into the mixer to monitor sound. You will need to check that the headphone jack of your mixer is the same as that on your VCR. If it isn't, the cheapest solution is to buy an adaptor. If you can, get headphones that will plug directly into the headphone jack of the VCR, and then use an adaptor with the sound mixer. An adaptor is more likely to work loose from the often crowded socket panel of the VCR than from the sound mixer.

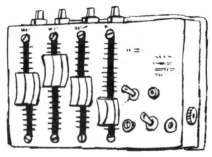

A simple 4-channel sound mixer.

Most sound mixers also have line inputs. These are necessary to mix sound from tape, disc, or another VCR. Line inputs can be used together with microphone inputs – for example, mixing a voice over with taped music. Some mixers can be connected to the microphone socket of the VCR, others amplify the audio signals to line level and must be connected to the audio inputs of the VCR. Connecting line inputs to the microphone input will seriously overload the circuits.

If a sound mixer only has line outputs, any one of them can be reduced to microphone level by inserting an attenuator (a reducer of signal) between the line output of the mixer and the microphone input of the VCR.

Some manufacturers offer custom designed 'sound processors', for stereo sound recording. These can be used for sound mixing, but they are mains only, so could not be used on location away from the mains. And they only have two microphone inputs, which you may find limiting.

HOW TO SHAPE SOUND WITH A GRAPHIC EQUALISER

Live and recorded sound is made up of varying frequency bands. These bands can be suppressed or boosted electronically with a graphic equaliser. Doing this, it is possible to compensate for poor acoustics, as well as to correct minor interference such as audio hiss and hum.

A graphic equaliser consists of a number of slider controls, each of which represents one band of the sound frequency (usually an octave). At the slider's middle position, the frequency band is unaffected by the equaliser. Setting the slider above or below the middle line shapes the frequency band accordingly. It is the shaping of sound in this way that is 'graphic' since the sliders when set in their various positions resemble the curved line of a graph. A simplified form of frequency response is provided by the bass and treble controls found on domestic audio equipment.

It is quite possible to use the graphic equaliser built into some domestic Hi-Fi systems for video work. Simply route the audio signal through the graphic equaliser on its way from the mixer output to the VCR. Be careful to keep left and right channels apart if you are making stereo or dual audio soundtracks.

Usually the graphic equaliser is used during, or after, two-machine video editing, rather than at the time of recording the original sound track.

MONITORS

There are two essential differences between a monitor and a TV. A monitor will not receive broadcast transmissions since it has no internal tuner. It will only accept pure audio and video signals. And the picture quality is superior to that possible using a TV. A monitor will give you a more accurate display of the true colour and contrast of the picture. This will help you set the camera controls more accurately. When editing, it will help you select the best picture to use.

Monitors, like TVs, come in a range of sizes for different applications. Some are designed to be used in TV studios, and can show picture only. Portable, battery-operated monitors are ideal for location work. A small monitor can be bought for about the same price as a portable TV. For a little more, you can have the best of both worlds and get a combined TV/monitor.

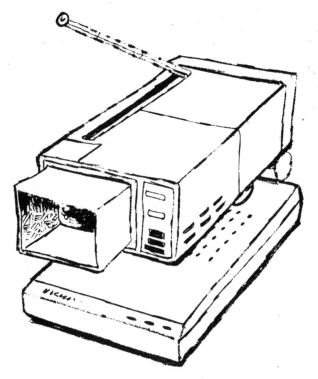

A portable, battery-operated combined TV/monitor.

A monitor uses pure video and audio signals to play back from the VCR, rather than the radio frequency signals used by the TV. This accounts for the better quality – the signal is pure. It does not have to be modulated and then demodulated (ie converted back and forth) by the VCR and the TV. Where a Euroconnector (also known as PERITEL) is fitted to both VCR and monitor, video and audio signals are carried within the same multiway cable, ie Video and Audio Out, Video and Audio In, all out of one socket on the VCR and into one socket on the monitor.

Otherwise two leads are required to make the connection: Video Out on the VCR to Video In on the monitor; Audio Out from the VCR to Audio In on the monitor. Video Out is usually a BNC connector; Video In on the monitor can be either BNC again, or phono. Audio Out on the VCR is usually phono, whilst Audio In on monitors is generally phono or mini-jack.

Check carefully what connectors or adaptors you will need to use the monitor. It is worth buying or making up special leads without using adaptors, as adaptors can work loose and become unreliable.

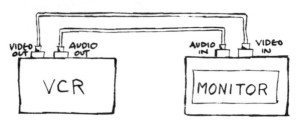

How to connect a VCR (Video and Audio Out) to a monitor
(Video and Audio In).

More sophisticated cameras have their own power supply, either from batteries or mains adaptor, and a Video Out socket, which can be connected directly to Video In on a monitor. This means you don't have to use a VCR when you just want to display a presentation or demonstration for a live audience, or where you are just rehearsing shots without wanting to record.

If a camera has its own power supply and a video output,
you can connect it directly to a monitor without using a VCR.

HOW TO PREPARE AND USE CAPTIONS AND GRAPHICS

Using captions and graphics is a very good way of making your videos look more professional. Particularly important is the title caption, which sets the tone for the whole programme. But, of course, the design and preparation of your captions has to be done carefully. Captions are the one item in a programme that you can have more control over than any other, as they can be prepared in advance of production.

The traditional way to prepare captions for television and video is to use dry transfer lettering, such as Letraset, on stiff card or board. The reason that Letraset has always been so popular is that it is quite easy to use, and gives good results, even if you have no artistic ability at all. As long as you can draw a straight line with a pencil and ruler, you can prepare good captions.

Dry transfer lettering is sold in sheets which provide a backing for the letters, and is widely obtainable in white or black. There are many different styles, and it is best to opt for one of the chunkier ones, like helvetica bold. You can also get a wide range of standard symbols. To get the best results, you must be careful and methodical. Draw faint guide lines across the caption board, which you will use to make sure that all the letters in one line are straight. Take care over getting the correct spacing between letters and words. A common mistake is to leave too much of a gap between words in a line, and between lines of words.

The letters are transferred by placing the sheet over the surface you are using for the caption, and rubbing over the required letter with a soft pencil. Use soft even pressure, and the letter will transfer to the caption board. It is best to work from the middle of each letter outwards. If you make a mistake, a letter can be removed by gently dabbing it with masking tape. The letter will come off, stuck to the tape. Don't apply too much pressure, or you will tear the surface of the caption board. Once the letter is transferred, it can be fixed by placing the supplied thin paper interleafing over the letter, and rubbing it with a smooth hard object on the letter you have transferred. The sheets do dry out over time, which makes the letters crack, so store them in a cool place, and don't buy more than you need to use over a short period.

All captions should be prepared to the same scale. The TV camera frame is slightly longer in width than height. The exact ratio is 4:3, width to height. So your caption boards should be cut to this ratio. A good size is 12″ × 9″: 12 inches wide by 9 inches

93

high. This is the correct ratio, and large enough to allow a safe area all around the lettering.

Because many domestic TV sets and monitors are overscanned, 10% or so of the picture area which is recorded onto tape is lost when it is played back. So allow for this in preparing all captions, and keep lettering well away from the edge of the board. This will also prevent the edge of the caption board coming into shot. To be quite safe, on a 12″ × 9″ caption, keep all your lettering within the 8″ × 6″ area.

*Captions must be designed so that lettering is
well away from the edge of the frame.*

Keep all captions simple. The fewer words there are, the more impact they will have. It is especially important to avoid detailed captions and graphics if a large number of people might view the programme. Some of them will have to sit a long way from the set, and will not be able to read small lettering on captions, or fussy graphics.

If you are using a sequence of captions, keep all the lines of words in the same place, or the lines will seem to jump around in the frame when you cut from caption to caption.

The lines of words should either start the same distance from the left edge of the board, or the lines should be centred. Centring is more tricky. You need to work out the number of words and spaces in each line, divide by two, and start from the middle letter or space and work outwards. All lettering used in captions in one programme should be consistent. You can choose to use capital letters or small letters, or capital letters for the first letter of the first word in a sentence. Using capital letters for the first letter in every word looks odd.

In general, white lettering on a black or dark colour background is most effective, as the letters will stand out in contrast with the darker background. Black letters on a white background are usually less effective, as the background is too prominent.

If you use colour captions, take care that there is sufficient contrast between lettering and background. Green and brown, for example will look too similar, whilst yellow and blue will contrast well. If in doubt about whether two colours will contrast well, use the black and white electronic viewfinder, or turn the colour down on your TV set. If the shade of the two colours looks similar, then there is not enough contrast. Don't use red in captions. Colour video cameras never reproduce red very well, which is why you rarely see a video picture of a London bus looking as it should!

You can add the personal touch to your programmes by drawing or painting your own captions. Don't make the work too detailed. Bold strokes will give a better effect. Whatever designs you come up with, make sure that they fit in with the tone of the programme. Cartoon-type graphics, for example, might look out of place in a campaigning video; on the other hand, humour can often make its mark where other methods fail.

Captions do not have to be made out of traditional materials. Some of the most effective captions I have seen have been produced using sand, split peas – and a bootlace! Magnetic letters work well, as does signboard lettering. Lettering machines give excellent well-spaced captions, and are very quick, but these are quite expensive.

You can get some interesting effects by using pictures and photos as a background to your captions – perhaps stills taken while shooting on location. The busier the background, the bolder the lettering must be, to stand out clearly. A simple effect to produce, but one that is most effective, is to make up your Letraset captions on clear film or plastic, like that used with overhead projectors. Using a photograph on a mounting board as the background, overlay the photos one at a time, and record them in sequence, pausing the VCR after each one. The captions will cut cleanly with the photo constant in the background. Take great care, though, not to move the camera or the photograph, and to align each acetate in exactly the same place. To help in this, use a permanent marker pen to draw fine guidelines in the four corners of the mounting board. Draw corresponding guidelines on each acetate sheet, taking care that they are in the same position on each sheet.

Use an overlay technique for a sequence of captions with a photo in the background.

Another simple way to change captions is to prepare them on a continuous roll of mounted paper or on card, attach it to a wall, and then, starting with the top caption, slowly tilt down. If you do this carefully, you can make it appear that the captions are rolling from the top of the screen to the bottom. A good sturdy tripod is a great advantage when attempting precision camera movement of this kind.

If you lay an overhead projector on its side, it is possible to use the rollers for a rolling caption effect, using either the OHP's own clear plastic roll, or a paper roll wound round the rollers. Use masking tape to fix the end to the roller itself. Thick paper or thin card works best for this.

If the caption is lit, it will read much clearer. Use only soft lighting, or if you use white lettering, the letters will 'bleed' into each other. On the other hand, if the background is white, it will glare. Centre the light source, so that the light falls evenly over the whole caption.

Make sure that the captions you prepare to use in a programme are all the same size. This makes handling easier, and you can even flip captions over or pull them away whilst shooting to get quite a good change-over effect. Some kind of caption stand is advisable. It must be secure and solid enough to hold the caption upright. A music stand might be sufficient for single captions, whilst an artist's easel would be fine for several captions. A children's blackboard set also makes an excellent caption stand!

Electronic captions can be produced using an electronic titler fitted to the camera or camcorder, or a computer. Since the lettering produced by these systems can be quite small, many people make the mistake of trying to fit too many lines in one caption. Also, you must be equally careful to keep all lettering within the safe area. Be extremely wary of special effects like zoom captions. If over-used, they will soon become tiresome and hackneyed. There is no substitute for a clear, bold, well produced caption, simply presented.

The timing of a caption sequence is important. The captions need to be on screen long enough for them to be read comfortably. But leave them on for too long, and you will slow the pace of the programme down. As a rough guide, allow 1.5 seconds per word for titles and credits, and up to twice that for factual information.

USING PRINTS, DRAWINGS AND SLIDES AS CAPTIONS

Photographic prints can be used very effectively in video. If the print is large enough, you can add movement by panning across the photo, and/or zooming in or out. Starting a shot with a detail and slowly zooming out to reveal the whole image can be most impressive. Rehearse the zoom out so that you don't over-zoom and show the edge of the photo. Mount photos on board, so that they lie flat when you're shooting them, or the picture will be distorted. This is a particular problem with a video light, which gives out a lot of heat.

It's quite possible to use gloss or matt photos as photo-captions, although you will find matt are easier to deal with, as they reflect less light. But most camcorders and cameras are able to pick up the finer quality of the gloss finish. The aspect ratio of a standard 35mm print is not quite that of the video frame, but near enough for most purposes. However, if the picture has been taken in such a way that its height is greater than its width, you will only be able to get about half of it in the frame without showing a picture edge.

Using the macro facility of a zoom lens, all sorts of printed matter can be used for captions. Newspaper extracts are particularly good when used in documentary fashion. Even typescript can be used for simple captions; the results are often better than electronically produced titles, as there is more control over positioning, background colour and lighting.

Using maps, charts and graphs can cause problems, if the

colours are weak, or the outlines are poor. It is often necessary to redraw this sort of material to use it effectively. You don't have to be able to reproduce a lot of detail; the simpler you can keep the design, the better the message will get across. If you are making charts, take a lesson from the days of black and white television, when patterns – diagonals, horizontals, and perpendiculars – were used to distinguish between categories. Using shape as well as colour will reinforce the differences you are trying to draw attention to.

Use the macro setting of the zoom lens to improvise captions from newspapers and typescript.

Some cameras have a negative–positive (negaposi) switch, with which it is possible to view negative still film in normal colour. To do this, the negative must be mounted in a holder, and the macro setting of the zoom must be used. Some manufacturers have their own custom-made adaptors. For slides, there are many different slide-transfer adaptors in the video accessory shops.

You could make your own adaptor for slides. Join two pieces of wood to make a right-angled frame, and cut a thin groove in the base and the side, just wide enough to hold the slide in place. Fix a large piece of white card on the wall, by a table. Put the frame about a foot away from the wall. Now set up a video lamp so that it shines directly on the white card, and is reflected onto the reverse side of the slide. This will give a bright enough image to record onto video. The same technique can be adopted with large-format transparencies. These are excellent for transfer to video, as their larger size will allow you to pan and zoom over the surface.

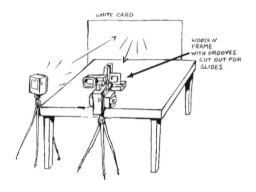

Slides and large-format transparencies
must be held securely in place.

When using negatives, slides, or film, you may well find that the usual white balance setting for the available light can be altered with improved results. Fluorescent light usually works very well as a light source for slide transfer; bright sunlight can also be used to effect. Be prepared to experiment if you want to get the best out of the camera. The principle always remains the same with all camera work – the more *you* can do the less the camera will have to do.

HOW TO TRANSFER CINE FILM ON TO VIDEO

The easiest way to transfer films (and slides) to video is simply to project them onto a screen or white wall, position the video camera by the projector, and record the projected image. The only problem is that the picture may be a bit distorted since the camera will be shooting at a slight angle. This effect can be lessened if the projector is placed below the camera, rather than to the side. Note that if the camera is too close to the projector, the motor can affect the video camera picture and cause distortion.

You can get better results by using a slide/film recording (tele-cine) adaptor, which reflects the image so that it can be shot head-on, so there is no distortion. Special glass is used to give a clearer, brighter picture, and some people use a silvered mirror to reflect the image.

Transferring moving film to video can result in a rolling bar effect or a flickering. The electronic fields which make up the video image are scanned (in the UK) 50 times a second.

8mm film is projected at 18 frames per second (fps). Projected through a three-bladed shutter, the speed of 8mm film is thus (3 × 18) 54 frames per second. The slightly faster speed causes the flickering.

Professional 16mm film is projected at 24 fps. A two-bladed shutter gives a speed of (2 × 24) 48 frames per second. Flickering is still noticeable, but not so bad.

Some projectors have variable speeds. A 16mm film must be projected at 25 fps to avoid flickering. This would reduce the running time of the average feature film by about 3 or 4 minutes! The faster running speed raises the pitch of voices etc, but the difference is so slight, it is not noticeable. On the other hand, an 8mm film must be projected at $16\frac{2}{3}$ fps. Here the sound difference often is noticeable.

Film made on 16mm for TV is usually filmed with cameras which shoot at 25 fps, so that the problem is avoided at source.

Another annoyance when transferring film or slides is that hot spots are common – intense bright projected areas which glare. These are a persistent problem, and you will need to be careful of tube burns if using a tube camera.

There is a technique of film transfer which does not use projection, and therefore does not suffer from these problems. It is called flying spot telecine. It passes a beam of light over the film while it is running. The colour and density of the film are interpreted electronically to build up video signals. However, this process is very expensive, due to the high cost of the equipment involved.

SIMPLE SPECIAL EFFECTS

There are a range of simple special effects that can be employed with video. You should consider carefully the purpose of the effect: does it assist the aim of the programme? You should never use a special effect for its own sake, unless, of course, you are simply experimenting. And overuse of any effect will soon become tiresome to the viewer.

Superimpose (i.e. overlaying one picture onto another, usually a caption over pre-recorded picture), and wipe (i.e. one picture gradually replacing another, appearing to push it out of frame) are very simple effects that can be achieved without specialised equipment. One makes use of the limited focal length of the camera lens for a kind of superimposed caption effect, the other uses a mirror for a wipe effect. But there are hundreds of other possibilities, using differing angles for the mirror, multiple mirrors, shooting through different shapes cut out of card. More bizarre ideas include smearing vaseline on a plain glass filter in front of the lens, and deliberately altering the white balance to get novel visual effects.

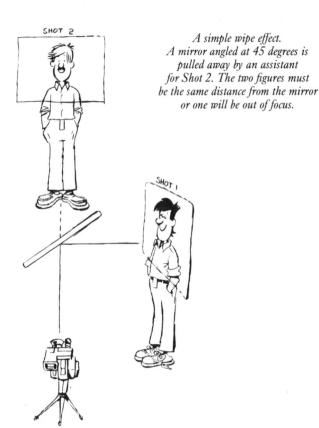

A simple wipe effect.
A mirror angled at 45 degrees is
pulled away by an assistant
for Shot 2. The two figures must
be the same distance from the mirror
or one will be out of focus.

If you take a piece of glass or clear plastic, write on it with felt pen, and then mount it 18 inches or so from the camera, you will be able to focus on the caption, whilst losing the background as a blur. If you then bring the background into focus by turning the focus ring, the caption will disappear from view. The trick will also work in reverse. These materials can also be useful for adding background detail in a shot – a popular method in old films.

For a simple wipe effect, position the camera pointing at subject B. At 45 degrees from the camera, in front of it and to the left or right, position subject A. By careful placing of a large mirror, it is possible to start recording subject A (as a reflection from the mirror), then pull away the mirror to achieve a wipe to subject B. Variations on this using other mirrors are only limited by your time and imagination.

HOW TO GET ELECTRONIC EFFECTS USING AN EFFECTS MIXER

Effects equipment used to be designed and priced exclusively for the professional market, but now there are a number of low cost, high quality and versatile effects machines suitable for the small-format user. These can be seen at some specialist video dealers, and many are advertised in the video magazines. As with all accessories, you should make sure that the effects equipment is compatible with your own video equipment, and that it does what you want it to do, before you part with your money.

The special effects that you are likely to find most useful are those that make the final production look more professional. These range from simple fades, to wipes, superimposition and colourisation (adding colour electronically to a caption originally produced, for example, with white Letraset) of captions. Most worthwhile effects rely on mixing images between two cameras, or a camera and a VCR.

However, there is a problem. Most camcorders and cameras are designed with their own picture synchronising pulses (ie they generate their own internal sync). One important effect of this is that you cannot use two together, cutting or mixing between them. Because they cannot be synchronised, the pictures will not be stable at the cut and mix points.

However, certain black and white cameras are designed to be driven by external sync, and can receive their synchronising pulses from the effects mixer. These can be used for superimposing captions over pictures from a camcorder or camera, or from another VCR whilst editing.

An effects mixer can be used to superimpose captions.

Captions can be made up from Letraset, for example, using black lettering on a white background. The caption is mounted, and the black and white camera connected to the mixer and focussed on the caption. The mixer accepts the image of the caption, reverses the caption electronically to white on black, colourises the lettering to any one of a variety of colours, and finally superimposes the caption on a shot from a second camera, or a VCR. Exactly where the caption is superimposed onto the main shot depends on where the caption is framed by the black and white camera.

The effect can be faded up and down using a slider control. It is also possible to reverse the effect, so that a shot from your main colour camera is keyed into the area of lettering or design shot with the black and white camera. Some effects mixers also incorporate horizontal and vertical wipes, and, more usefully, basic sound mixing facilities.

Two cameras cannot be used together into the same VCR without some means of synchronising them, which is called genlock. Cameras with genlock can be used in multi-camera production with effects mixers. Switching, mixing and wipes are possible between the two cameras, although adjusting the cameras to align with the mixer, and matching each camera's colour saturation and contrast, is a job only to be tackled by a technical expert. These camera signals cannot, however, be mixed with those from a VCR without the use of a time base corrector (TBC) to standardise the VCR's unstable sync pulses. A TBC is an expensive piece of equipment: in fact not all industrial and commercial video units have one.

WHEN TO HIRE EQUIPMENT AND WHAT TO LOOK OUT FOR

Assuming that you have your own basic video equipment, there might well be times when you will want to hire additional equipment or accessories. For example, you might want to hire a better camera than the one you normally use to video a special occasion, or to get a higher quality origination. Or you might just want to hire a battery belt for a lengthy location shoot. Your first port of call should be one of the video workshop and media groups where you will find not only equipment hire at a reasonable price, but also help, advice and training.

Commercial hire costs vary greatly. Various factors come into play, including the durability and cost of the item when new. It's always worth shopping around, too, as prices vary quite a lot from place to place. But it's never worthwhile going somewhere where the equipment is below standard. Reputation and recommendation are a good guide; you can also get a fair idea of the likely service you will get by a general impression of how organised the company is and how helpful they are.

The great advantage of hiring is the obvious one – that you only pay for equipment that you use, and you don't have expensive equipment lying around unused. The disadvantage is equally obvious: cost without ownership. But hiring equipment as you need it means that you can choose the right equipment for each job, and you are always able to choose from the latest available technology. For example if you normally prefer to use a tube camcorder, because of its high resolution, you might consider hiring a CCD or MOS camcorder for making a video of a summer aerial display.

Hire first, before you buy a major piece of equipment. The only way to be sure that an item of video equipment is going to be what you want is to try it out in your usual working conditions. Sometimes this can be arranged by the dealer who is selling it to you, who will then deduct the hire charge from the purchase price if you subsequently go ahead and buy.

Equipment hire is always covered by a hire agreement. These are usually exceedingly long and over-complicated, and make you liable for all sorts of eventualities. One of the key things to check for, though, is when you are contracted to return the equipment by. Hire charges are usually per 24 hour day. Sometimes you can arrange slightly earlier collection or delivery, depending on your schedule. Don't take liberties though. Always negotiate any alteration to the normal terms, and expect to pay for another day's hire if you return equipment the following day, or keep another hirer waiting around.

Whenever you can, book your equipment hire well in advance, and confirm the day before, as even the best companies make mistakes sometimes. If you have never used a company before, check what deposit will be required, what identification you will need, and what parking arrangements are like nearby, particularly if you are hiring much equipment, or if it is heavy. Try to arrive in good time so that you can check the equipment and test it out before you take it away. The hire shop should always let you do this, as you *will* be held liable for any malfunction or damage on return. If you have never used the equipment before, ask for a demonstration. It is all too common for people to hire out, say, an advanced camera, and then find on location that they can't operate it. Also check simple things, like the connections, and whether they are compatible with your own equipment, or whether an adaptor will be required.

If you intend to hire your equipment to others, then amongst the things you have to consider are how much the hiring will interfere with your own use, the risk of damage, and insurance against loss, damage and breakdown. Unless you can afford to have the equipment out of action during repair, or to replace it, you ought not to hire your equipment out.

The high cost of professional edit suites makes hiring a popular option. They can be hired with operator/technician in attendance ('wet hire'), or self-operated ('self-op' or 'dry hire'). Rates are usually quoted per hour, half day or day.

HOW TO USE A COMPUTER WITH VIDEO

Computers have been used for some time in broadcast and industrial television to store and carry out editing commands, and to generate graphics. Their use is now becoming far more widespread, and there are graphics programmes available to run on popular home computers.

You have to be aware, if you are considering using a computer for titling, that its signal output *may* not be suitable to link direct to your VCR. Remember that the highest quality input to a VCR is achieved by a pure video signal. That signal is comprised of sync pulses, which synchronise the picture, vision and colour information. Together, these different elements are called composite video – sometimes also called encoded video.

Some computers have a composite video output, in which case they can be linked directly to the Video In socket of the VCR.

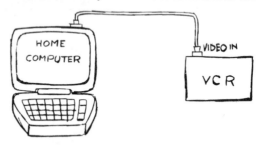

How to connect a home computer directly
to a VCR using composite video.

Computers often have an RGB output, designed to be linked to the special computer monitors. These signals cannot be fed directly into a VCR. They need an encoder, so that they can be encoded to provide a composite video signal. The third signal type you might come up against is RF. Here if the RF signal itself was not to be used, a demodulator would be required to convert the RF signal to composite video. Happily, however, a composite video output is the norm, and certain computers now available which are designed for use with video, have a composite video output to connect to VCRs. The BBC Micro has RF, RGB and composite video outputs.

Assuming that you already have a home computer, the cost of graphics programmes, which are available on tape or floppy disk, is low. This method of producing graphics can be considered a reasonable alternative to in-camera electronic titling. However, not all of the computer systems can superimpose the output of the computer onto moving images recorded from the main camera or the VCR. For example, to do this with a BBC Micro you would need to add a genlocking board. This allows the Micro to synchronise with the VCR. If you have a system that can't superimpose electronically, the only option left to you is to do it optically, by using an effects mixer, pointing the caption camera at the monitor screen, and superimposing the output over the main shot. Apart from problems caused by screen reflection, you would lose quality and definition of image doing it this way.

WHY AN EDIT CONTROLLER IS USEFUL

If you need to set up two VCRs for two-machine editing, the procedure is the same as for copying from VCR to VCR. Editing is, after all, fundamentally a matter of copying video between two VCRs. However there are edit controllers available which make the editing process more automatic, and which allow greater accuracy and flexibility. The basic edit controller cues up the two VCRs at edit points you have pre-selected, and then controls the actual edit.

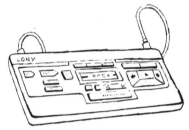

An edit controller, which will control edits between an 8mm VCR and any other VCR format.

Edit controllers will only work with specified models, although there is some compatibility between badge engineered VCRs, that is, clones made under licence by another manufacturer. The one illustrated here, designed for the 8mm format, will also edit between 8mm and VHS or Betamax. On this version, edits can be previewed, so it is possible to see the effect of an edit before committing yourself to recording it. This is a significant step forward in small-format editing.

WHY YOU NEED TO BE CAREFUL WHEN SENDING TAPES ABROAD, OR PLAYING BACK FOREIGN TAPES

Standards conversion *may* be necessary to play back a tape recorded overseas.

In television and video, there are three colour systems used in different countries: PAL, SECAM and NTSC.

PAL is used in the UK, Europe, (except France), and much of the Commonwealth and former colonies.

SECAM is used mainly in France, USSR and other Eastern European Countries.

NTSC is used mainly in USA, Canada, most of South America, and Japan.

PAL and SECAM are 625 line standards, replaying 50 fields per second, and tapes can be played between these two systems, although the picture will be black and white only. NTSC is a 525 line standard, replaying 60 fields per second, and thus completely incompatible with either PAL or SECAM.

It is, though, possible to buy multi-standard VCRs and monitors, which can be switched between one system and another. However, there are further differences within single standards (eg SECAM Vertical and SECAM Horizontal), which could still prevent you replaying a particular tape. And of course, you will still need to check that the format of the VCR (VHS, 8mm, etc) is the same.

A more straightforward solution is to have copies made which are simultaneously converted from one standard to another. This is called standards conversion. Note that as with all copying or editing of videotape, standards conversion will result in some loss of quality.

Creative Production Techniques

Now a closer look at the creative part of making videos. You should be familiar with the operation of your camcorder or camera. You should also be able to follow a moving person by panning and tilting, allowing looking room and headroom for the shot. The next stage is to give some careful thought to the choosing of shots.

If you are not editing, but assembling a sequence or programme in-camera, then pre-planning is all the more vital. Each shot must be carefully considered before you start recording, because if you make a mistake, even if the action *can* be repeated, you still might be in trouble. Every time you re-record a scene, you have to record over a fraction of the end of the previous shot, to make sure that the faulty take is completely recorded over. This could spoil the pace of the previous shot, or worse, you could accidentally record over the last word or two, or some significant action.

How long to hold a shot is a matter of pace, continuity, visual interest, and feeling. Each new shot should have a purpose, and in some small way should advance the action. Perhaps a series of shots of two people having an argument, that gets more and more heated, could get faster as the shots get tighter and the argument reaches its climax. On the other hand, a shot with plenty of movement in the frame may provide enough visual interest for you to use fewer shots. There are no hard and fast rules as to how long a shot should be. It depends on what it has to do.

Deciding the best camera angle involves more than choosing the best viewpoint. The frame of the shot is rather like the frame of a picture, and so what the frame contains must be balanced. The shot must appear in proportion. Artists study composition to ensure balance and perspective in their paintings, and a good book on how to paint landscapes and figures is essential reading for the budding programme maker.

There are, however, a number of useful guidelines to composition which can be applied to most shots, which will help you avoid making basic errors.

It is better not to position your subjects in the centre of the frame, but slightly to one side, if you can. Dividing the frame into thirds is one of the classic methods used to compose well-balanced shots. Placing the significant parts of the subject at the intersections of the thirds is a useful guide to improve your awareness of picture composition.

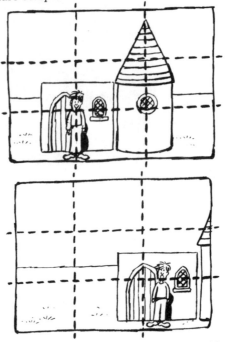

Use the rule of thirds to help get balanced composition.

Try to avoid a head-on shot.
It makes the subjects look flat and ordinary.

Using the division of the frame into thirds is just one method of achieving balance in your shots. A straightforward way of balancing a shot is to put two subjects an equal distance from the centre of the frame. However, if that were to be shot head on, the shot would be too symmetrical and uninteresting.

If you track left or right, to angle the camera, you will favour one or other subject, or one or other aspect. If the shot looks un-balanced when you are taking a view from an angle, try tracking, or zooming in and out slightly. You can also achieve a balance by framing the subject nearer to the camera more to the centre of the frame, and the further subject more to the edge of the frame.

*Put one subject in the foreground
to make the shot more visually interesting.*

Next, look at the shape of the shot. Not just the subject, but the background. What direction is your eye led towards? If there are vertical or horizontal lines in the shot, then the eye is probably being led *away* from the main subject. This will work against you, because you are aiming to get your viewer to look *at* the subject.

*Avoid horizontal and vertical lines
which distract attention away from the subject.*

Diagonal lines can be equally distracting, but their presence can often make the shot more interesting if they are not *too* vivid.

*Make use of lines in the frame to draw
attention to the subject.*

As well as zooming and tracking, you can also vary the height of the camera to alter composition. Remember, though, that doing this will affect how the viewer interprets the shot. For example, in a drama, a low camera angle may imply that the subject is powerful, or dominating, or simply very tall.

HOW TO USE VISUAL LANGUAGE

Most of the shots you will need to compose, however, will not be in the nature of a landscape or a still life. As well as understanding the principles of framing and composition, you have to come to terms with objects and people that move. As well as the need to re-compose the shot while recording, you have to build up a visually meaningful sequence.

There are a variety of interesting techniques and approaches you can take. As an example, suppose you want to record a sequence where a girl gets off a bus, walks along the street, suddenly stops, realises that she has left her purse on the bus, and flags down a passing taxi. She gets in the taxi, and the taxi drives off after the bus. That scene might be part of a video you were making, using two friends to play the parts of the girl and the taxi driver.

How do you approach shooting this scene? After finding a suitable location, do you place the camera on the bus stop side of the street or the other side? Most probably you would opt for the bus stop side, as then you would be able to see her actually getting off the bus, and later getting into the taxi. Where would the best place be for the camera? It you wanted to show her expression as she realised her purse was missing, then the camera must be placed further along in the direction she will be walking. That will give a clear view of at least three-quarters of her face.

Place the camera so that there is a clear shot of the action.

From position A, you could shoot the whole scene as a wide angle shot – but that might lack interest. A mixture of shots is better for variety.

You can choose any position as long as you stay on one side of the action only. If you shoot the girl walking along from position A, and you cut to her walking from position E, the girl will have appeared to have changed direction. This would give confusing information to the viewer. It is called 'crossing the line' – an imaginary line known as the line of action. In this case, the line is that formed by the girl walking. All the positions A, B, C and D can be intercut, E cannot – it crosses the line of action.

Camera position E crosses the line of action.

If you frame a two-shot, the line of action is the line running between the two subjects.

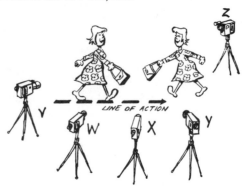

Cutting to position Z from the others
will make it seem as though the subjects have changed position.

For dramatic emphasis, perhaps include a close-up of her face as she realises her purse is on the bus. As far as showing the approach of the bus is concerned, you have a choice of starting the shot with the bus, which would be a dramatic opening to the scene, or establishing the scene first, allowing the bus to drive into shot. Which approach you take will depend on what the last shot was, and what impact you want. The second way is smoother, and will appear more controlled.

If you wanted two shots of the bus approaching, one as a wide angle, the other as a medium shot, showing the girl on the platform ready to get off, you could either zoom into the medium shot, or cut between the two. A zoom might emphasise the point that she is on the bus, but it is very hard to do well. A cut would be the usual way, but you may not have time to set up the second shot. And if you are assembling the sequence in the camera without editing, timing the beginning of the second shot would be difficult.

One solution is to take your wide angle shot of an earlier bus, but taking care not to show the number plate, or any other distinguishing features, such as adverts. That would give away the fact that it's not the same bus when the two shots are seen one after the other. Another way of concealing the deception is to make the second shot a tighter medium shot, so that only part of the side of the bus is in shot, in such a way that it could be any bus.

This manipulation of reality and of time is fundamental to working with the moving image. Think forward to the likely next shot after we see our distressed girl getting in the taxi. It might be a wide angle shot of the bus and the taxi, showing the taxi catching the bus up. At the start of the sequence, the taxi might not have arrived at the bus stop for 30 seconds or more, as you would have needed the time to show the girl leaving the bus, looking in her bag, and so on. By cutting from the girl getting in the taxi, to the bus and the taxi together, you will have compressed time. The viewer will not even realise it. Compressing time is a visual convention which we all accept. The device is used every day on television and in films. It is used because it would be boring to show every part of the action, and it would also make programmes extremely long.

Compressing time is not a difficult technique to use. What you have to make sure of, though, is that you don't confuse the viewer. There is always an implied link between the shots you cut together. Such as from the girl getting in the taxi to the taxi catching up with the bus. Think of the conclusions the viewer would draw if you then cut to a shot of a man jumping off the bus and running off. The man would be linked with the purse – he must have stolen it. But if you had simply shown a man running, then the link is less obvious, and the shot could be confusing – he might be running for the bus.

A shot should never confuse the viewer. This applies to cuts within a sequence, or between one sequence and the next. Vary the shot size or the angle of view, or both, to maintain visual continuity. If you introduce a new person into a scene, then you need to shoot a re-establishing shot (RS) to show the relationship of the newcomer to the person or persons in the original shot.

Shoot a re-establishing shot (RS) when someone new enters to show their relationship with those already in the scene.

HOW TO MAKE THE BEST USE OF TUNGSTEN-HALOGEN LAMPS

Using just three or four tungsten-halogen lamps can dramatically improve the quality of the video image. People come to life on video when they are properly lit. They appear more three-dimensional, facial features are more readily noticeable, hair is highlighted, and textures in clothing can be brought out. To get these effects it is really necessary to use a number of lamps, and to place each carefully. The commonest problem is that each lamp you use, because they are so powerful, will cause a shadow – both on the subject's face and on the surroundings. And more than one shadow will look quite odd, and spoil the effect you were trying to create.

If you use just one lamp from behind the camera, this will improve the picture, and the shot will appear much brighter, but it will also be rather flat. The shot will still be two-dimensional. However, one lamp is frequently used by ENG (electronic news gathering) video crews. For a crew of just two or three people it is often the only way to get enough light onto the subject. More lights would need more people to hold them, and there often isn't room or time to set them up. This demonstrates an important rule in video – that you have to be flexible and practical. Seldom will all the theories work out in practice!

If you do have control over time, and the setting of the shot, then by using more than one lamp, you will be able to bring out facial features, and create realistic effects. If you have just two lamps, place one each side of the camera. One needs to be a strong spot light to illuminate the shot (i.e. a 'key' light), the other a softer flood to fill out the shadow on the face caused by the spot (i.e. a 'fill' light). For a better effect, add a third lamp behind the subject, or bouncing off a background wall, to separate him or her out from the background, and to sharpen the outline of the head and body (i.e. a 'back' light).

The intensity and distance of these lamps will have to be varied to find the ideal balance. If you have all three lamps available, set up the key and fill lamps first, arranging the back last. To avoid shadows on the background set the key lamp as high as possible. This will also give a more natural appearance to the shot since in everyday life lights shine *down* on us. If there's room, it also helps to move the subject away from the background, so that any stray shadows from the key or fill will fall on the floor, out of shot. If you have a fourth light available, it can be used to light the background, which will emphasise it, and further separate the subjects.

3-point lighting is used to give the shot more depth.

It is possible to use daylight through a window as a key or fill light. So if you only have two lamps available, you can still manage to set up 3-point lighting. But you would have to compensate for the mixed lighting. Use an orange gel over the window, or a blue gel in front of the lamps, to match the colour balance. Gels will reduce the overall lighting level, so carefully check in the viewfinder or on a TV or monitor that the shot is adequately lit when the gels are in place. Alternatively, if you have a manual colour balance control, careful adjustment to the red end of the spectrum might compensate. Trial and error is the best approach.

To light groups of two or more people, the best way is to try and use the same key light and back light for them all, with side fill lighting as necessary to deal with shadows. Reflectors can often be used effectively to provide full lighting for two-shots.

Lighting larger areas is a matter of using available light, or making a sizeable investment in several powerful lights. It is often possible, though, to limit the action to one smaller area at a time, re-setting the lights you do have as you move from shot to shot.

If there is a light-coloured ceiling, you may be able to get away with simply pointing all your lights upwards and bouncing the light onto the subject(s). Reflected light causes far fewer shadow problems than direct light.

HOW TO GET BETTER SOUND FROM MICROPHONES

Good sound quality depends upon a large number of factors, all of which interact to contribute to how faithful or distorted your sound quality will be. There are well-established guidelines, but, of course, each sound recording is unique, with its own particular set of factors that will influence it.

A good overall rule is to keep it simple. If you use two microphones where one will do, you run several risks. There are twice as many microphones to go wrong! Putting the microphones too close together will distort the sound. They should be three times as far apart as each is from the subject.

Keep microphones well spaced apart or the sound will be distorted.

Two or more microphones used together have to be in phase, that is, their polarity – the order of wiring – must be identical. If they are not, the efficiency of the microphones is severely impaired.

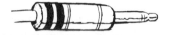

Mini-jack audio connector.

Standard jack audio connector.

Using two or more microphones also involves careful balancing of each one. Each speaker should be given equal 'presence' – that is, each should be at their correct distance from their microphone. Fine adjustments only should be made on the sound mixer. It is not reasonable to expect a mixer to compensate for poorly placed microphones. Increasing the level of one channel will also increase the level of background noise. If you try to edit shots featuring each microphone alternately, the ambient sound levels will be unbalanced, and you will lose continuity.

Have the microphone in shot, directly in front of the speaker, whenever possible. Hand-held microphones that are specially designed to be used in shot tend to be slimmer in appearance, and given a neutral, matt finish so that they are non-reflective and unobtrusive.

For drama, and other situations where the microphone would be inappropriate, you have to seek the best compromise. Frequently the answer will be to use a gun microphone, held by an assistant just out of shot. As it is so directional, it is essential that the operator monitors sound using headphones. Then any slight movement off-microphone by the speaker can be compensated for.

Gun microphones require power, either from a sound mixer, a separate battery pack, or their own internal battery. Some have a pistol type grip attachment to make hand-holding easier. Aesthetic considerations may make you decide not to use a gun microphone in shot, as the necessary wind shield trebles the width all along the length of the tube. The microphone can often be held safely and more comfortably below the frame, rather than to the side or above it. This position also avoids shadow problems in sunlight or when using spot lamps. Attach the microphone to a short pole if necessary, although don't underestimate how heavy this can become when held at arm's length.

Holding a gun microphone at arm's length
can be very tiring!

If personal microphones are worn in shot, they can be attached to a dress, lapel or tie. If it is not worn on the tie, it should be attached to the same side the speaker will be facing. The cable can be taken over the top hem of a dress and then down inside the dress, or into the front opening of a blouse or shirt. The cable should be secured by tape or tucked into clothing before running away from the speaker, so that there is no danger of it being tugged if the speaker moves around.

It is also possible to conceal a personal microphone under clothing if required, either hanging around the neck, or taped to the upper chest. Care must be taken that clothing is not allowed to rub on the microphone, as the sound will almost certainly be picked up. This is particularly bad with synthetic and shiny fabrics.

Sound quality can often be better in the open air, rather than indoors. Indoors, the acoustics are seldom ideal for recording video – hard walls and floors readily reflect sound, giving a resonant echo to the sound. Whilst drapes, soft furniture, etc, all help, that particular problem can be avoided altogether by going outside. And of course, lighting is often better outside, too.

But there are other problems in outdoor locations. Because there is no reflected sound, the microphone must be held closer to the speaker to compensate. And you may well find a higher level of background noise – traffic, machinery, birds, pedestrians, and so on. A particularly loud background noise may require a directional microphone to cut it out, whereas more general background noise will be more effectively dealt with by an omni-directional one.

You should aim to record sound onto videotape as loud as you can without distortion. Whilst the audio level meter on a mixer, or VCR if fitted, will give some indication of sound level, the only sure and safe guide is to do a test recording and play back through a good quality loudspeaker. That excludes most TV loudspeakers. Of course, this is impractical to do on location, and for every change of microphone position and scene, but once you have practised doing several sound tests in this way, you will soon learn what is the maximum audio level you can achieve for different types of recording.

HOW TO ORGANISE A PRODUCTION

Organising a production involves more than getting video equipment sorted out. There are many other things that you need to take account of. If the video is commissioned by someone else, then you will probably be given a deadline to meet. That becomes the starting point for working out your schedule.

The schedule is a series of deadlines, ie dates when different jobs have to be done by. When working out the schedule, it is best to work back from the programme deadline. This may be the shooting day itself, or later if you are subsequently adding voice-over, music, or editing the programme. If you are working on a programme only in your spare time, then the schedule can easily be spread over a longer period. When you are shooting, those days will have their own schedule, or running order, which will be determined by the order in which the shots are to be recorded.

Note that the shooting need not all take place on successive days. If you are editing, it is quite usual to record over a longer period, fitting in with the other demands on the time of your presenter, and access to locations.

The schedule is a working document, and a copy should be given to everyone involved in the production. Any changes must be notified to everyone. It is a good idea to date all schedules and scripts, so that it is quite clear that everyone is working to the latest version.

If you are making a video for someone else, for example, a wedding video, it is vital to establish exactly what the client wants. And to establish who the client is! If you are being paid, then your duty is to the payer. You must provide what is wanted. If it is edited highlights, then it is no use providing a two hour record of everyone and everything. Having said that, a complete record of everything is, in fact, what many people do want from a wedding video. But either way, you need to find out first, and make sure that the client knows exactly what you are going to provide.

For a local community or voluntary group, company or other organisation, you would usually be expected to provide a fairly detailed treatment, specifying the aim and objectives of the programme, showing how it was going to be shot, the general tone and style, the sort of locations, the kind of things that would be said, and so on. It is better to prepare this with the client's co-operation, to avoid frequent redrafting and amendment. Making your treatments as detailed as possible will improve your chances of a successful production.

HOW TO WRITE A SCRIPT

Writing a script may sound rather daunting, but really all it involves is thinking about what you're doing beforehand. It helps to clarify what you want to do and the best way to achieve it. If you don't do this, then you'll end up with lots of material on tape that you can't use. You don't have to know in advance exactly what's going to happen in order to write a script. A script can be just a framework – you can organise the details when you arrive on the scene.

A script is a system of setting out the words and pictures that go to make up a programme, together with technical information such as camera shots and shot numbers. Having a well set out script is invaluable, because it makes recording much easier than trying to work without one. The script will show when everything has to be done, and in what order.

If you are assembling a programme by shooting in sequence, then your script sequence will be the same as your shooting sequence. If you are editing, you will probably be shooting out of sequence, but the script is still vital to have on hand to make sure that you have continuity between shots.

You can approach preparing a script by starting with the words or with the shots. Whichever way you choose, be sure to decide first what the aim and target audience is. Write these down, and bear them in mind all the time you are scripting.

The script extract which follows is an imaginary one. It is known as a presenter script, as it contains only the words that will be spoken

> The library service is just one example of the many facilities which are being cut back in our borough.

> The opening times here have been cut by 20% since the start of the year. People have had to put up with these conditions since before the first world war. In February, work was supposed to have started on modernisation. That's now all been shelved.

> This would be a familiar sight to anyone who uses this route regularly. It'll take on average about 24 weeks to repair this. That's twice as long as anywhere else in this part of the country.

The minutes of the Council meeting held on 3rd June don't provide much comfort either. . . .

The first thing that you will notice is that it is all printed on the right hand side of the page. That makes it quite clear what words are actually going to be spoken in the programme.

The left-hand side of the page is where all the visual information will go: shot numbers, shot sizes, and any special instructions to the camera operator.

DEBORAH (VOICE-OVER)

6	/The library service is just* one example of the many facilities which are being cut back in our borough.
MS TOWN HALL DOOR (EXT) *SLOW PAN L TO 'TOWN HALL' SIGN	
7	/The opening times here have been cut by 20% since the start of the year. People have had to put up with these conditions since before the first world war. In February,/work was supposed to have started on modernisation. That's now all been shelved.
MCU SWIMMER IN POOL SLOW ZOOM OUT TO W/A POOL	
8	
CU RUSTY SHOWER FITTING IN WOMENS CHANGING AREA	
9	/This would be a familiar sight to anyone who uses this route regularly. It'll take on average about 24 weeks to repair this,/That's twice as long as anywhere else in this part of the country.
MS POTHOLES IN GEORGE ST	
10	
BCU POTHOLE	
11	/The minutes of the Council meeting held on 3rd June don't provide much comfort either. . . .
WA TOWN HALL; PAUL IN FOREGROUND	

This complete script with shots and words is sometimes called a camera script. You need to know some simple rules to be able to read a script.

Each shot is numbered above the line, and all shot information and speech is written below the line. Thus, all the information between the first two lines refers to shot 6, and so on. Study the format carefully and you will see that it is well designed for practical use – all the information you need to know about any shot in the programme is collected together in one place, to the right and left of the page.

At the end of each horizontal line separating one shot from another is an upward stroke. This stroke shows the exact cutting point between one shot and another. If the upward stroke is placed in the middle of a sentence (as it is in shot 8), we know the precise word after which the cut should occur.

In shot 6, there is a note for the camera operator to pan the camera left at the point marked * in the presenter's script. The purpose of the * is to ensure that the precise point when the pan is required is not left open to doubt.

If you can it is clearer to type the script. Make sure that all alterations are notified to any others involved in the production; you don't want the crew working to different scripts!

A good script is the basis of a good programme. Try to follow these guidelines to make your scripts more interesting:

1. Scripts are spoken, so write for the spoken word. This means using everyday language. Don't be afraid to write the way people speak.

2. Use a portable cassette recorder. If you find writing scripts that sound natural is difficult then visit the locations and record your views and impressions. If someone else is providing the content, talk to them on tape. This will give you a resource of spoken language on which to base the script, and it may also save you from having to wrestle with someone else's script.

3. Keep it short. A major fault of many scripts is that they are too wordy. You are writing for a visual medium. Let the shots speak for themselves, and don't repeat information that the viewer can see perfectly well on the screen.

4. Be direct. Avoid jargon and flowery language and, in particular, avoid phrases like 'as you can see. . . .'

5. Make it interesting. Don't stick to the obvious and the ordinary. Avoid patronising the viewer. Don't shy away from difficult issues, or be frightened to set out all sides of an argument.

6. Write for one viewer. This will help to keep the style relaxed, personal and conversational. Keep the target viewer constantly in mind. Use references and language which will relate well to him or her.

7. Try to develop your writing style. No language is neutral. Be aware of the emphases that you are placing in your scripts.

Sharpen your writing so that each script you write has a characteristic 'feel' to it.

8. Research locations carefully. The scene you are presenting to the viewer must be matched by the script. For example, a very noisy location will not lend itself to a script containing long and involved analysis.

9. Keep to one subject. Don't try to cover too many points in one programme, or your viewer will drown in detail.

10. Use examples and contrasts in your writing. Your script must aim to trigger the imagination, as well as expanding upon what is shown on the screen.

11. Change it. Don't be too proud (or too lazy) to alter a script if you or someone else comes up with a better idea. If you're not sure, write a draft script first, which can be used as a basis for analysis and discussion. Number each draft to avoid confusion. Your presenter may well want to change words and phrases if he or she finds them a problem.

12. Read the script aloud. This is the only way of checking that it sounds OK. Read it to yourself and to your colleagues. Record it on sound tape and play it back.

HOW TO PLAN A PROGRAMME THAT WILL BE EDITED

Having access to a second VCR for editing will mean that you can be more creative in the way you use video material, and more flexible in the way you shoot it. In effect you are free to shoot out of sequence and assemble the programme later. Assembling the shots together, one after the other in strict sequence from the beginning to the end of the programme, is called assemble editing. Assemble editing can be done between most VCRs with little, if any, picture interference at the edit points. Connecting the VCRs is done in the same way as tape-to-tape copying.

Editing allows you more leeway to make mistakes in shooting, and gives you more scope, than sequence shooting. If you're recording a shot, and you make a mistake on camera, for example, you don't have to cue up the tape at the end of the previous shot, and re-record over the mistake. You can record the same sequence again – and again, as many different times as you like. You are free to take different angles, different shots, and to use different ideas.

125

Decisions on the sequence of shots in the final programme can be left until the editing stage. Live sequences can be intercut with captions and graphics. Voice-overs and music can be mixed onto the edited version. You can re-use material that you might have used in other programmes.

With all this choice, where do you begin? The best way is with the script. In an unedited programme, the script is how the programme will be shot. Shot 1 will be recorded first, followed by shots 2, 3, 4 and so on. In an edited programme, the script shows how the programme will finish up, after editing.

So to plan a programme for editing, you need to work out a shooting sequence. That is a list of the order in which you're going to record the shots. Sometimes the shooting sequence will be decided by geography. Obviously it makes sense to record all shots in one place together, during one visit.

The shooting sequence can also be influenced by when people are free to appear in your programme. And captions and graphics may need a certain time to prepare before they can be recorded – or they might be edited direct from the camcorder or camera. Also, some equipment may be available only on a certain day, such as a hired camera, microphone, or battery pack.

When you have decided the best shooting sequence, you are free to concentrate on planning the shots themselves. Programmes are built up of a number of scenes, each of which needs to be shot in the most visually effective way. The pace of a programme depends not only on the variety of shots, but also on taking the viewer forward with the action, and developing each scene carefully.

Shooting for editing is quite different from shooting in sequence. When shooting a video that will be edited, you must shoot a run-in at the beginning, and a run-out at the end of each sequence you record. If you use an edit controller, you should allow fifteen seconds run-in to a shot to synchronise the Play and Record VCRs. Also allow ten seconds run-out at the end of each shot. If you are simply using two machines to edit, without an edit controller, you will still find the run-in valuable for timing the edits more accurately.

Another difference is that you are going to be shooting more than you will need for the final programme. And at some point, after you have finished shooting, you will have to sit down with a notepad and choose what shots to use. If you have recorded a shot more than once, for example if you make a mistake, or shoot the same sequence from a different angle, each new recording is called a 'take'. Writing down all the shots and takes is called 'logging'.

TAPE NO	SHOT & TAKE	TIME	DESCRIPTION	COMMENTS
1	4/2	13'06"	MS JOHN	CAMERA SHAKE
1	5/1	14'06"	CU BUS STOP	GOOD
1	6/1	15'45"	CU JOHN	GOOD
1	7/1	16'20"	PANL OVER BOAT	GIRL SHOUTS
1	7/2	16'55"	—— " ——	GOOD

A log sheet, partly filled in for editing.

You can use the VCR tape counter for rough logging, but the more accurate way is to log in minutes and seconds. The easiest way to do this is to load the tape, rewind it, and set a stop-watch to zero. Start the tape at the beginning and start the watch at the beginning of the first shot (after the snow). Keep the watch and the tape running, and note down the time at the beginning of each new shot.

If your editing is going to be done on a hired edit suite, do the logging at home beforehand. Your logging will be accurate enough as long as you log in minutes and seconds from where the control track starts on the tape, and you have not left any gaps between shots and takes.

When you shoot for editing, you may well record several times more material than you need. This is termed the 'shooting ratio'. If you record three times as much as you are eventually going to use, your shooting ratio is 3–1. Even if your shooting ratio is only 2–1, finding your way around the different takes, and distinguishing the good takes from the 'out' takes, can be a headache.

To get round this problem, it is a good idea to record some identification at the beginning of each shot and take. This is normally done by holding a board in vision, called an 'ident' board, as it identifies the shot and take number. The shots are numbered as per the script, the takes are numbered in ascending order – Shot 1 Take 1, Shot 1 Take 2, Shot 1 Take 3, and so on. The first time you record shot 2, that will be Shot 2 Take 1. You can buy ident boards ready made, or you can simply use a small blackboard. The ready-made ones have spaces to chalk in the title of the programme, the date, director and camera operator's names, shot and take numbers. In shooting film, they are called clapper boards – the clapper is to synchronise sound and vision – which is not required when you record both together in video.

The ident board must be clearly chalked before each take, with the shot and take number. Once the VTR has started to record, the ident board is held in shot whilst you call out the shot and take number, and count down, out loud, from 10 seconds, before you cue the action. This should ensure you have 15 seconds or so run-in to every shot and take.

*An ident board in shot saves a lot of time
when logging and editing.*

This will speed up your editing, and help to stop you using the wrong take in error. If you forget to board a shot at the beginning, hold the board upside down at the end of the take. That means that the board information refers to the previous take. This is called end-boarding.

The idea of counting down from 10 out loud is a good one. It makes sure that everyone knows you are recording and the take is about to start. It also makes things easier when editing, as it helps to cue a take at the beginning when required. If you pause the edit VCR when you hear 'ten' you know that you have ten seconds, plus cueing time before the start of the take itself.

Editing with video allows you the luxury of overshooting – over-lapping action at the beginning of the shot. There is always the danger that when you cut together two shots of the same person, they might be in a slightly different position. A jump cut (where the subject appears to 'jump' in the frame) may result, even if the two shots are a different size and from a different angle. You can avoid this by re-shooting the last piece of action of the preceding shot. You will then have the same action recorded twice, but from a new angle or shot size. Now you can make sure, when you edit, that the transition is continuous. You also have a choice of the precise cutting point, which can be invaluable for setting the right pace or dramatic tone.

Don't leave gaps between shots and takes. The more continuous the recording (and so the control track), the more accurate your logging will be. Use backspace editing while shooting to butt up all your shots and takes.

Varying the shot size and angle from shot to shot, and shooting overlap are two primary ways you can ensure continuity when you edit. This demonstrates that editing starts before you record the first shot. You need to develop the technique of shooting for editing.

Editing also has implications for how you light your shots, and for sound. When you are planning what shots will go together in the final edit, you need to make a separate note of any possible lighting or sound continuity problems. For example, a straight cut from a shot of a hearth and the glowing embers of a fire to a sea view on a summer's day would entail a stark contrast in lighting between the two shots. All other impact would be subordinate to the difference in colour balance between the two shots.

Similarly, you need to be careful about shooting in the same location at different times, or on different days. If the shots are edited together, the lighting continuity must be preserved.

If you do want to edit two shots together where the colour balance is significantly different, the best way is to start the second shot with a close-up, where the visual discrepancy would not be as great.

The same principle applies to sound recording. Sound levels must be matched from shot to shot, so that there are no major differences in sound level from one location to another. For example, if you were post-recording questions to edit into an interview, any significant differences in sound level will be immediately noticeable. Careful monitoring of sound levels is important, as is taking a written note of any particular sound problems that might affect editing, such as aeroplanes or other extraneous sound.

Once you have assemble edited a programme, you can't replace part of a shot you have edited with a new shot. If you try to do this, there will be several seconds of picture interference at the Edit Out point. This is because the control track of the inserted shot will be out of sync with the original at the point where you want to return to the original, master shot.

An insert edit is an edit which is inserted into a master shot. The Edit In point is where the insert starts, and the Edit Out point is where the insert ends. Unlike assemble editing, insert editing does not replace the control track on the tape in the Record (Edit) VCR. A flying erase head leaves that part of the tape intact. This is why it is possible to replace part of a shot with a new inserted picture. The Edit Out point, which is when you return to the master shot, is as clean as the Edit In point. Because the master erase head is not being used, the original soundtrack can be retained. You can replace a whole shot after a programme is edited, using insert editing, but of course, timing has to be exact. It is easier to time the exact Edit In and Edit Out points with an edit controller, which allows you to preview the edit before it is recorded on the Record VCR.

Once the control track is recorded onto a tape,
insert editing leaves it intact.

If you have insert editing, it is advisable to use it for all your editing. A continuous control track is more electronically stable than one which is assembled shot by shot. So your edits will be cleaner, with fewer glitches. To record a continuous control track, record with the lens cap on. This will produce a tape with black level and colour burst, which is essential synchronising and colour information. You need to record for the whole estimated length of the edited programme, plus several minutes extra as a margin of safety.

Start insert editing one minute after the start of the black level, which will normally be one minute into the tape. The control track, laid when you recorded black level, will remain intact, providing a continuous sync reference for more stable playback and copying.

Insert editing is very useful indeed. You can, for example, shoot a scene using a wide-angle shot the whole time. You can then shoot a number of other shots of different size, and from different angles. These can replace the wide-angle shot as required. The continuity of sound is taken care of because the soundtrack is left alone – you are only changing the pictures. You could think of insert editing as dubbing vision instead of sound.

You do, of course, have to make sure that you observe visual continuity. The principle is exactly the same as when shooting in sequence or assemble editing. You must not cross the line of action, and you still have to avoid jump cuts. The shots that you will record for inserting during editing are generally called cutaways. When you edit, you will cut away to the new shot – and then cut back again to the main shot. Cutaways are the most useful shots you can record in an edited programme. Always record lots of them. Cutaway questions and reaction shots are used to maintain visual continuity when editing interviews.

Editing places considerable strain on tapes. Before editing cutaways, do a clean wind. This will make sure that the tape is evenly tensioned, and that there are no kinks in it.

Avoid jump cuts when you edit cutaways. Change the shot size, or the angle of view, or both. Changing angle is less effective in avoiding jump cuts if the two subjects are in a similar position near the centre of the frame. Also watch out for objects, apart from the main subject, in successive shots. They can appear to jump in the frame.

Complementary to the cutaway shot is the cut-in shot. As the cutaway cuts away from the main action, so the cut-in shot cuts into the main action, usually to show detail within a wider angle shot. An example would be a medium shot of a woman reading a note followed by a cut-in of the note itself, then back to the MS again.

Cut-ins and cutaways can be used to give life and atmosphere to a scene. In choosing these shots, you ought to try to think of what the viewer's eye would want to see in the shot. In a busy scene, for example, interspersing W/A and MS shots with cutaways of snippets of action and detail helps to add realism, thus making the scene more interesting. The most challenging part is the creative bit – going beyond the ordinary elements of a scene to highlight the particular aspect you want the viewer to think about.

Cutting between Shots 1, 2 and 3 would cause serious jump cuts;

Shots 4, 5 and 6 vary the shot size
and so can be cut together without making the
subject appear to jump in the frame.

Cutaways and cut-ins should be lit with great care. Lighting for those must appear to be from the same source as the master shot. It is as important to take care of visual continuity from the technical side as it is from the aesthetic side. Breaks in visual continuity in either respect will weaken the viewer's interest in your programme, as well as your reputation as a programme maker!

Master shot A; Cut-in shot B.

HOW TO SHOOT AN INTERVIEW

It is important to have the interviewer and interviewee (respondent) in the right places to shoot an interview. You should aim to show as much of the respondent's face as possible. Place the interviewer slightly in front of the camcorder or camera. The respondent sits or stands opposite. There are then three shots available. The over the shoulder (OSS) two shot, or the single shot, which is usually medium close-up (MCU) or close-up (CU). Each shot will show the respondent to the best advantage, almost full-face, looking slightly to one side of the lens.

If you are not going to edit, then you should start with the OSS, and slowly zoom in to the MCU or CU during the first answer. Then stay on that shot for the whole interview. It may be tempting to zoom in or out, but if the interview is interesting, the viewer's attention will be held by the content.

An edited interview is approached in rather a different way. You don't have to use any answers you don't want to; they can be cut out. To preserve continuity, re-shoot some of the questions. These new shots allow you to alter the length and sequence of the interview without losing continuity.

Start as for the un-edited interview. Once you have an MS or CU, you can hold that shot for the whole interview, change the single shot, or pull right out to the OSS again. Each time, the zoom should be done during the question.

Now shoot the cutaway questions. Re-shoot all those that were asked while you were changing shots, and any other important questions. You can re-shoot the questions in two ways. Either re-position to where the respondent was sitting or standing, and shoot them from the reverse angle (cutaway A), or simply change angle slightly, framing the interviewer in a close-up (cutaway B).

Cutaway A   *Cutaway B*

*Two ways of shooting cutaway questions
for edited interviews.*

133

Cutaway B is quicker, makes use of the existing lighting set-up, and will look OK as long as the background is out of focus, or looks slightly different from that in the answer sequences. Either way, make sure that the interviewer's eyeline is consistent with the respondent's eyeline. If you're not sure about whether the eyelines match, or whether the background looks different enough, replay the tape and check.

The eyeline in the noddy shot B
must match the eyeline in the master shot A.

Next shoot cutaway reaction shots, or noddys. These are shots of the interviewer just listening, or nodding slightly, as though listening. For variety, also shoot some OSS 2-shots, of the interviewer just talking to the respondent. As long as the interviewer is in profile, and the viewer can't see exact mouth movements, these shots can be insert edited over questions.

Watch continuity as you conduct the interview. Don't let the respondent take off, or put on, clothes, specs, or anything else. Remember you may want to use the pictures if it's a good interview, and you also may want to change the order if you edit. The edits could make it look as though the interviewee is continually dressing and undressing. For the same reason, don't allow cigarette smoking – editing could make the cigarette appear to shrink and grow from answer to answer!

Editing an interview is a matter of timing and feel for the subject. To look natural, the timing of the edits has to be quite precise. Don't include too many cutaway questions or noddies, or the editing will be too obvious. Watch out for continuity on the OSS 2-shot, especially if the interviewer and respondent are seated (leg-crossing, arm-folding, etc).

Further editing of the interview can be done when it has been cut to the required length, and all the cutaway questions and noddies are edited. Other cutaways, on subjects raised in the answers, can now be shot, and inserted as required into the edited interview.

HOW TO EDIT SOUND

There are numerous ways in which the soundtrack of a programme can be changed and improved. The most straightforward way is to use audio dub, which replaces the existing soundtrack completely, and adds a new one.

You can use audio dub effectively in programmes which feature various sequences where the sound is mainly ambient. That means that the sound is background only (a 'wild track'), with no particular or specific sound source. This could apply equally to the countryside, or in a busy street. Traffic noise when recorded onto video all sounds pretty much the same. Once you edit such sequences together, you may find that the sound 'jumps' between cuts. This happens because although background sound is similar, the levels at different points are slightly different. And cutting between one shot and another may show up this difference.

The solution is to record over the edited soundtrack using audio dub. Take a sound tape recorder out with you when you record a sequence involving ambient sound, and record while you are shooting. As long as you have recorded enough to last the whole programme you can use it to replace the original soundtrack.

The next step is to connect Audio Out of the tape recorder to Audio In of the VCR. Cue the effects tape on the sound recorder slightly before the start of the ambient sound. Cue the VCR slightly before the start of the edited programme. Start the VCR and tape recorder together. If you have audio level controls on the VCR, fade up the sound of the tape recorder, watching the screen for the start of the programme. You should monitor the level using headphones, but you can get away with using the TV or monitor loudspeaker, as you are not using a microphone, so there won't be any howl-round problems. At the end of the programme, fade out the sound, as this will give a pleasing completeness to the soundtrack, making for a more professional effect.

If your VCR doesn't have audio level controls, you can connect the tape recorder to the line input of a sound mixer. The line output of the mixer can then be connected to the audio input of the VCR. You can now fade the effects in and out at the beginning and end of the programme.

However, if you are recording a commentary or voice-over after you have finished shooting (post-production), then straight-forward audio dub should be avoided. The snag is that atmospheric sound ('atmos') or ambient sound as it is sometimes called, is vital to a soundtrack. Each location has its ambient sound – countryside, factory, school, on a bus. Recording a voice-over in a quiet room to add to such scenes would lack atmosphere, and sound 'dead'.

So the question is how to mix the new soundtrack – in this case the voice-over – with the original soundtrack. On VCRs which have two audio tracks, you may be able to audio dub new sound onto one track only, leaving the other with the original soundtrack intact. Playing back both tracks simultaneously will automatically mix the two tracks. The main problem with this method in practice is that it is hard to match the sound levels of the two tracks.

An alternative is to mix the tracks while assemble editing a shot. It involves using a sound mixer. The Play VCR feeds into the mixer, together with the voice-over microphone. The ambient sound from the Play VCR and the voice-over from the microphone are mixed together, and connected into the Record VCR. The new soundtrack and the picture are recorded on the Record VCR at the same time during the assemble edit.

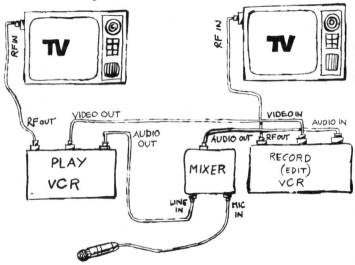

How to mix voice-over and taped
ambient sound during the assemble edit.

This method can be used for both one and two soundtrack VCRs, but it is only suitable for a sound mix which is contained entirely within the shot being edited. For extended mixing of new and original sound, for example where the voice-over is to accompany several shots, then a different method must be used. The sound mixing must be done after assemble editing has been completed.

A straightforward way of doing this is to assemble edit the whole programme to a second VCR, mixing the new and original sound as above. But as you will then have a third generation tape, picture quality will be poor.

An ambitious solution is to record the original soundtrack onto a tape recorder, and then re-record it onto the VCR again, mixing in the new track. To do this, connect Audio Out from the VCR to the Line input of the tape recorder. Cue the VCR at the beginning of the programme, and record from VCR to tape recorder. When this is done, connect the tape recorder to the line input of the sound mixer and the voice-over microphone to the microphone input of the mixer. Then audio dub is used to re-record the mixed soundtrack back onto the VCR.

The problem with this approach is the difficulty of cueing the tape recorder and VCR at *precisely* the same point for laying back the sound, and also the slight variation in speeds of the tape recorder and the VCR, which will cause the sound to be slightly out of sync.

For some sequences, the slight difference will not matter, because it will not be noticed. The most common difficulty is where you have someone's lips in shot as they are speaking. It is obviously important to match lips with words, as even a slight delay in either will be very noticeable. Matching lips and words is called lip sync. It is vital to retain lip sync, and the slight mechanical variation in the speed of the two machines is usually enough to lose lip sync.

One approach is to avoid the problem in the first place. Plan your programme in such a way that you do not have people speaking to camera. Another way is to re-lay the mixed soundtrack in brief segments. The longer the segment, the worse the sync problems become. With care and lots of patience you may be able to keep sync over a short run of tape.

If your sync problem is only momentary, for example someone claps their hands in shot, or slams a door in shot, you could use a cutaway shot to record over the give-away picture of the clapping or slamming.

A sophisticated way of keeping sync between a VCR and a sound tape recorder is available, though. Good specialist video dealers can supply an electronic video sync device which connects to the VCR and uses the electronic sync pulses on a recorded video tape to control precisely the speed of a modified sound tape recorder. Having recorded the original soundtrack from VCR to sound tape recorder, it is re-laid via a sound mixer, together with the new soundtrack. The soundtrack will be in exact sync with the original programme.

If you add a stereo sound recorder, or two mono sound recorders, to your system, it is possible to mix a number of different soundtracks together onto sound tape before transferring them onto video by any of the above methods.

Using a stereo tape recorder, which has two soundtracks, 1 and 2, you could record a voice-over onto track 1. Then rewind, and record music on to track 2. Both sound channels can be replayed at the same time.

With two mono tape recorders, you can build up a composite soundtrack by recording from one to the other, adding a new track each time.

Many different combinations of live and recorded sound can be built up, using tape recorders together with a mixer, recording from one tape to another. Audio from a VCR can also be mixed onto the soundtrack. The main point to watch is continuity – keep the soundtrack in sync with the pictures all the time.

If you are using one of the tape-to-tape methods of sound mixing for voice-overs, you must ensure that the voice-over is recorded at a strong level, so that the increase in tape hiss usually present when recording from one tape to another, is kept under control. If you can, try to feed all sound sources, via a sound mixer, into the VCR at one time. The less tape-to-tape transfers involved in getting the final master soundtrack onto the VCR, the better the sound quality will be.

HOW TO RECORD A VOICE-OVER AND BACKGROUND MUSIC

Background music should be added to the programme after all the editing has been done. The programme must be edited into its correct running order first, so that the music fits the final version.

Voice-overs are also recorded in this way, although if you have a pre-recorded voice-over, for example a speech or narrative, it is quite possible to 'cut' the picture to the voice-over, using insert editing.

Scripting a voice-over requires some skill. The voice-over should complement and supplement the pictures. A good voice-over is punchy and to the point. It should not unnecessarily repeat things the viewer can see quite clearly on the screen. It should be smooth and well-paced. You should allow the pictures to establish themselves before coming in with the voice-over. The trick is to watch the TV or monitor as much as possible, and take the timing from the screen.

If you want to try out a voice-over before recording it on video tape, you can get a rough guide to the combined effect of voice-over and pictures by simply recording it onto sound tape, and playing back at the same time as the programme.

Try and use a room with good acoustics for voice-overs. Don't forget to take the phone off the hook, and warn others not to come in whilst you're recording. Any microphone can be used, but the omni-directional microphone is the best to use, as it will work well close to the mouth. Don't place the microphone on the VCR itself, or you will pick up vibration; it may also pick up the sound of the motor if it is placed too close to the VCR. It is safest to place the microphone away from the VCR and pointing away from it. Don't forget to turn down the volume control of the TV or monitor, or you will get audio howl-round.

Adding music is usually done from tape, as it is easier to cue accurately, but it can be done directly from disc. Or, of course, live! Sound from any line source – tape, disc or another VCR – must be fed to Audio In on the VCR. You can do much with music to influence the mood and pace of the pictures. A music background should be recorded at quite a low level. Only featured music should be recorded at full level. Certainly if you are mixing music with speech, the music must be lowered right down, so that the words can be clearly heard. Otherwise, far from adding atmosphere by adding music, you will simply lose the viewer's interest.

The simplest way of mixing music and voice-over together is by playing the music in the background whilst speaking the voice-over into the microphone. This can be connected direct to the microphone socket of the VCR, or via a sound mixer, or onto sound tape.

More Video Ideas and Projects

Differences between 'professional' and 'domestic' equipment are becoming more blurred. So are the distinctions between amateur and professional. There is now a new category – 'semi-professional' – which can apply equally to equipment, and those who use it. TV and video, once the preserve of those within the soundproofed walls of broadcast companies, is now available for everyone, not just to watch a diet of what is meant to entertain and inform us, but to use the medium in a more obviously active sense.

Small-format equipment is more sophisticated than ever. Features like insert editing and dual soundtracks, once found only on large-format video like U-Matic, have now arrived in the High Street. Access to broadcasting air time is still unbelievably restricted, but there are chinks in the armour, and some broadcast commissioning editors have started to look further and wider.

For those who are committed to small-format video, as a low-cost and creative medium, all this is encouraging. The technology of small-format video is no longer a barrier to it being accepted everywhere. From a technical point of view, there is no reason why small-format video cannot be used to master programme material for closed-circuit, cable, regional and national broadcast television, and satellite TV.

Not that you could go out and make a series of programmes, take them up to Television Centre, and sell them to the BBC. Not yet, anyway. But there are many other avenues for your work. If you are set on broadcast television, then experience gained using small-format video will be very valuable. It could certainly give you a head start on any production training courses. Many of the skills required for programme-making are the same for small-format and large-format video, and film as well.

For many, the next step forward from using video purely as an interest or hobby is to accept a commission to make a video for someone else. This might be to make a wedding video, or a training tape for a company, a sales promotion for a product, or a record of a meeting. As long as you approach the job in a conscientious and organised way, there is no reason why you shouldn't charge a professional fee for your work. In return, you must therefore provide a professional product.

WHAT IS INVOLVED IN ACCEPTING A COMMISSION TO MAKE A PROGRAMME

The first step is to be realistic. It would be unfair both on yourself and on your client to agree to make a video which was beyond your scope – either in terms of equipment or ability. The safest thing is to do a couple of test runs first, before you accept a commission. Many of the problems you may come up against may not be obvious. For example, you don't want egg on your face by turning up to video a wedding, only to find that the vicar will not allow a video camera inside the church. If you know about this in advance, then you can plan for it. Explain to the client that for the ceremony, you will have to edit stills with a sound recording.

Planning and preparation, or research, are vital to all videos, not least when you are accepting a fee. The research must start with what the client wants. For example, for a sales promotion of a product, how many people will watch it, and what kind of people are they – sales people, line managers, customers? Will they be given any other information with the tape, or will the tape have to explain everything? Does the product need to be seen on location, or in a number of locations? If so, where? How long must the tape be – how much time will be available to view it? Will there be someone there when the tape is viewed to answer follow-up questions? What is the aim of the programme – to sell the product, to inform the sales force of its features and benefits, or to impress the managing director?

You must take a thorough brief from the person who commissions you. When you think you have understood what is required, go away, write down in outline what you understand to be (a) the aim, and (b) the target viewers. Send this back for confirmation or further discussion. Once the aim and target viewers are sorted out, then you can go ahead and suggest ways in which the programme might be done. What sort of format, what locations, who might be in it, the general tone and style. This is called a treatment, and again, it needs to be carefully discussed and agreed before your camera leaves its box – even for the simplest of programmes. For example, you are making a video of Jenny's birthday party. Her dad is paying you to make it. You shoot three hours of video, go away, and produce a beautiful edited version which has storylines, dramatic cuts, special effects. All dad wants is the original tape. Everything you've shot, in the order you shot it. His treatment, not yours.

For more complex programmes, you might be asked to supply two treatments, for different budgets. This often happens because a programme is needed, but budget approval has to wait for a board meeting, so the options have to be kept open. For your part, you must be careful to cost everything realistically. Include all your own expenses and those of anyone working with you. Include a figure for equipment depreciation and overheads, and decide what your profit margin will be. If, when you add it all up, it sounds too high, keep your nerve. Don't ask, don't get. But remember that you are working in a free marketplace, and someone is round the corner who will do it for less. Maybe not as well, but more cheaply. Your trump cards are to have some work to show to your prospective clients and, longer term, to establish a reputation for the quality of what you do.

If there will be a demand for a large number of copies of the programme, then it is in your interest to keep the master tape, so that *you* can make and sell the copies. In many cases it pays to lower the production fee, agree to retain the master, and charge separately for copies. For weddings and the like, costs are then shared between a large number of people. If you can sell enough copies, you needn't charge a production fee.

If your client is a company or other organisation, it is usual to get some of the fee in advance. This is your guarantee against not being paid a thing if the programme does not go ahead through no fault of yours. Since the most time-consuming part of a production is researching and writing the script, it makes sense to ask for ⅓ payment on commission, ⅓ on delivery of an agreed final draft script, and ⅓ on delivery of the edited master and/or agreed copies. Use a letter of agreement, which will formally bind both you and your client to the terms you agree, prior to starting work.

All programmes rely, in varying degrees, on the co-operation and assistance of other people. To acknowledge, at the end of a programme, that help has been given, is a courtesy which is often neglected. Such an acknowledgement will go a long way in getting goodwill for you. Acknowledge people who help with the production itself, as well as any outside co-operation you receive. For anyone who has been really helpful, send them a complimentary copy of the finished programme.

HOW TO MAKE A CAMPAIGNING VIDEO

Video is an ideal medium to use to get a message across – using pictures and sound to persuade people to your point of view. Advertisers use this power daily. TV advertising is the most expensive of all – because it has the largest audience, and because it works. Each shot in an advert is carefully selected, each word must justify its place.

The success of a campaign video, in common with an advert, can be measured directly. The yardstick is whether the campaign succeeds or not. This may not be a very accurate yardstick, but it is better than none at all. In industry, videos are now made for both management and unions on key issues like redundancy, health and safety, conditions of work. Community groups use it to argue their cases, and many other groups find video has given them an effective voice.

If you are planning a campaign video, you must get the right 'angle', or approach. There is no such thing as a neutral programme. By choosing a shot, you leave others out. Editing of content takes place whatever pictures and sound you record. You will be using documentary technique. But the balance of humour, seriousness, fact, opinion, reportage and impression are in your hands. And you must decide how much editorial control you retain over what you produce.

Campaigns involve issues which people feel strongly about – traffic pollution, the lack of a creche, the closing of a law centre. As a programme maker, you can make use of this strength of feeling. An effective approach is to use a variety of location shots which illustrate the issue. In the case of traffic pollution, you'd want shots of congestion, loud noise levels, exhaust emissions, pedestrians' anxiety as they try to cross the road, potential danger spots, and so on.

Then you need to get people speaking. Ideally people with differing involvement and commitment to the campaign. Many campaign videos fail because they are *too* consciously slanted. A better approach is to present the issues, lean one way or the other, but leave the viewer room to differ. A hard-sell is not only counter-productive, but it usually makes for a boring programme.

The most natural way to get people to talk is to talk to them and record what they say to you. Don't allow them to talk directly to camera. As a documentary style, that is too didactic particularly where the presenter is expressing strong views. Either use the talking shot ('talking head') as it is, or use it as a sound overlay to location shots. Generally a mix of the two techniques is most appropriate. The exact balance will depend upon how long the programme is, and the subject matter. You can also shoot special cutaways when you have done the interviews, which can be inserted if you have insert editing available.

Screenings of campaign videos should be well organised. The video might be aimed at a small audience, for example a local council committee, or a large one, like a tenants' association. You may have a choice between public screenings, and individual viewing. Public screenings need to be well advertised. Set equipment up early, and check that everything is working, and properly tuned in. Everyone should be able to see the screen and hear what is said. Allow for a maximum of twenty people per average-sized set. If you have a larger group, place monitors or TVs back to back, so that people can see only one screen. If they can see more than one, the impact of the programme will be lessened.

Position monitors and TVs
back to back for large audiences.

Avoid using large-screen TV: the picture quality is poor when used with small-format video.

It is possible to arrange less formal screenings at meetings, conferences, exhibitions, and other places where a potential audience might be passing. Some VCRs can be programmed to play and rewind a programme continuously, without someone being there to operate the controls.

Other alternatives are to arrange individual or small group screenings, and to loan the tape for home view. This may involve having the programme transferred to another format. Packaging does not have to be elaborate – a simple label with the title, producer or production company, and running time. Break off the erase protect tab at the back of the cassette so that it can't be accidentally over-recorded. It's all too easy to leave a tape in the VCR after watching it. With front-loading VCRs, the label will be out of sight once the tape is in the VCR. Don't neglect to keep strict records of who you have sent the tapes to, or who has borrowed them. Apart from keeping track of your tapes, this information is important if you are going to monitor the success of the programme.

HOW TO RECORD MEETINGS ON VIDEO

Making a video record of a meeting is usually simply a convenient way of recording what took place, for the benefit either of the participants, or those who could not be present. It can portray the atmosphere in a unique way, and provided reasonable care is taken over pictures and sound, it will be a reliable record.

The main problem with recording meetings is that even the most organised ones have their own unpredictable momentum. For the camera operator, it can be extremely difficult to know who is going to speak next. He or she has the choice of forever panning around from speaker to speaker, or trying to get a wide angle shot of everyone! Without a wide angle lens, some sort of compromise is inevitable.

Sound can also be troublesome. Often large rooms and halls are used, where the acoustics are poor. A boom operator, who can direct the microphone on a pole towards whoever is speaking is ideal. Failing that, use two microphones, covering half the room with each. Keep them well spaced apart, and mix the sound through a sound mixer.

If the meeting is being chaired, and a video record is central to the aim of the meeting, then he or she can direct proceedings, taking recording needs into account. Speakers can be asked to wait until the microphone can be passed over to them before they start speaking. Usually, though, meetings have their own momentum, and the video is the last thing that is thought about.

Be there in good time. Make sure you have enough extension leads, and that your microphone cables are long enough. All cable runs should be taped to the floor or walls with strong, sticky (gaffer) tape, so that people don't trip over them. Choose your camera angle carefully. Take lighting into account. If it is insufficient, strong bounce lighting is best for this event. The farther you can be from the participants the better. You will still be able to get reasonable close-ups, and the farther out you are the wider the camera angle that will be available to you for discussion.

If you are going to edit the tape, and you can insert edit, shoot plenty of cutaway reaction shots: people listening, clapping, laughing, scratching their nose, or whatever. These inserts can be inserted wherever you need to shorten a contribution, or cut to a different speaker, or just to show audience reaction, approval or disapproval. Many of the techniques for shortening interviews can be employed when editing a meeting video.

Whether you edit a meeting tape or not, you don't have any choice but to keep recording the whole time. You can be sure that if you stop recording, you will miss the most interesting or dramatic contribution of the day! If you are not working on mains, then use a battery belt or pack, or you will have to change batteries every half hour or so. Change tapes at convenient breaks, so that you don't run out of tape at an important moment.

If the tape is edited, you will have every opportunity to prepare some captions after shooting. If you are sequence shooting, the title caption(s) must be prepared and shot beforehand. If you have an electronic titler, work out your captions beforehand and call them up as required to superimpose over picture at the beginning of the meeting. If there are only a few main speakers, it may be possible to store all the names of the speakers and superimpose them as they are speaking. Name captions need to be in shot for six seconds – remember, six and out. A simple but effective title caption can be made using the company brochure or logo as a background. One or more captions can be shot using the overlay technique.

HOW TO SHOOT DRAMA

It is feasible to set a video camera up in a theatre or hall, and simply record an amateur production using a wide angle shot. Many groups adopt this approach, and find it useful for record and publicity purposes.

To prepare specifically for video is more challenging. TV is more intimate than theatre, and an adaptation for video must reflect this. Close-ups are necessary to involve the viewer. The wide angle is too distant and impersonal for intimacy. The TV viewer is not actually present; there is no audience atmosphere. The treatment of the drama for TV must compensate.

One approach is to shoot a performance two or three times. Once to get a master wide angle shot. A second time concentrating on close-ups. And a third time concentrating on cutaways. The exact balance of these will vary depending on the type of drama. Generally, though, the more you can use the close-ups and cut-aways, the more impact the adaptation will have.

If you can arrange special performances for video, then scenes can be set up specially for shooting. You may want to hire personal radio microphones for each actor and actress, feeding into a sound mixer. Otherwise, sound will be a major problem. A gun microphone with an operator is the next best solution.

A more ambitious approach is to make two or three simultaneous recordings on separate portables. Pre-plan what shots each will take. Feed sound into each VCR, otherwise the slight differences in running speeds of different machines will make it impossible to keep lip sync when editing.

Ordinary theatre lighting should be sufficient for most camcorders and cameras to work in. The ideal shooting position is centre stage, at, or slightly above, the performers' eye level. If you are making two simultaneous recordings, you can vary the angle, but beware of crossing the line. Take care also to match the eyelines. You must cross-shoot to get full-face shots with matching eyelines.

Cross-shoot with two camcorders
to get full-face shots and matching eyelines.

WHAT VIDEO HAS TO OFFER FOR THE TEACHER AND TRAINER

In education and training, video has had a dramatic impact. Video is used in a range of subjects to bring learning alive. Real life situations can be brought into the classroom, using a medium which has a high acceptability amongst pupils. In the workplace, video training is an established part of many companies' programmes when new staff join, or when new skills have to be acquired.

Interactive video, which links video tape and videodisc with computers, is also attracting much attention. Using videotape, many imaginative learning programmes have been developed where the order in which you watch the video is controlled by a computer programme. This allies the memory and storage power of the computer with the enhancement of the video pictures and sound. Viewers take their own path through the programme. Which route they take will depend on what responses are made to prompts which appear on the video screen or the computer screen. Many such programmes are designed so that each answer is monitored and recorded, giving the instructor, at the end of the session, a print-out summarising the number of correct and incorrect responses, time taken to answer each question, and questions where more than one incorrect response was given.

Interactive video programmes which make use of videodisc are even more powerful. Videodiscs replay a very high quality video image. They have two full soundtracks, for stereo, dual level or dual language audio. Laser discs can reproduce a perfect still frame without any wear on disc player or disc, since there is no physical contact between the two. Search time between any of the 55,000 video frames on one side of the disc is about three seconds. Programmes can consist of any combination of still frames, and moving sequences. This is the system being used for the BBC Domesday project.

The potential of video extends beyond education and training programmes and interactive video. Those applications rely on pre-planned production of images, sequences and whole programmes. But less formal uses of video have even more educational value. Immediate record and playback is the crucial element. For example, it enables a group doing role-plays to watch a replay immediately the role-play has ended. This is of value in encouraging them to examine their own attitudes, opinions and behaviour in given situations. The value of this cannot be overestimated. In the hands of a sympathetic teacher or trainer, real self-evaluation can take place – far more than when relying on memory alone. The session must, however, be taken seriously by all concerned.

It may be preferable not to have other disinterested people in the session. You do not really need anyone to operate the camera. It can be locked off as a wide angle shot.

Video is used widely in training for public speaking, making presentations, how to interview, how to be interviewed, negotiation skills, management techniques, customer relations, and so on. All these applications make use of the record – replay capacity of video. Most often the recordings themselves are not intended to be kept. For training in sensitive areas, it is often better to assure the group that the tapes will be erased at the end of the session.

The activity of making video itself is educational for those involved. It teaches the need to plan, to communicate ideas, to work in a group, to accept a given role, to work to a common goal, to keep to a schedule, to use technology, to see a project through from beginning to end. The individual production skills necessary to make a programme are valuable in themselves, and applicable to other media apart from video.

HOW TO SHOOT A SPORTS EVENT

Shooting with a single camcorder or camera is rather restricting when it comes to shooting a sports event. A single wide angle shot is the safest method, but there may not be enough detail visible. If you try to follow the action, the amount of movement will be a strain for the viewer after a short while. The best approach is a compromise. For example, for football and rugby matches divide the field of play into four segments from end to end. Then get as much of the segment where play is taking place in the frame as possible. Only pan when play is about to enter the next segment. Thus you will have only four basic positions. This should cut down movement, and help the viewer to follow the action.

If you can insert edit, shoot cutaways of the crowd, and cutaways of players not involved in the action. You can use these to edit down a whole game into edited highlights. If you record a wild track of separate crowd noise on a tape recorder, this can be mixed in over the edits to conceal the difference in sound between two edited shots. When the teams change ends, either show it, or use a caption, for example, 'second-half'.

The best position is directly in line with the half-way line. The higher you can get the camera, the better the angle will be, and the more the viewer will be able to see. Some grounds have a large clock in view of the crowd. If you are editing, avoid getting it in shot, or your edit points will be obvious for all to see.

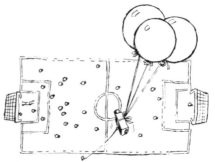

For sports events use a high camera position level with the half-way line.

It is most important not to cross the line of action when shooting sports events. If you do, you will confuse the viewer as to which way the teams are playing. The line of action runs between the two ends of the pitch. You can safely shoot anywhere on one side of the pitch without crossing the line: you can also go behind the goal (or the stumps) for a head-on shot. If you are shooting track athletics, pan with the athletes as they run around the bends. If you cut from the near straight to the far straight, when you edit the two shots, it will appear that they have suddenly changed direction.

HOW TO MAKE A MUSIC VIDEO

If you want to make a music video, it is essential to have insert editing. Without it, it is impossible to get the precision of editing necessary for the pictures to work with the music.

You need to start with a master soundtrack. If the music video is to include shots of the artist singing, or the band playing, then record a master shot of the whole number. This should be a wide angle shot, recording picture with sound. This will be your master shot, into which you will insert edit cut-ins and cutaways. Once the master shot is recorded, you need to get the band to play the same number again, as closely as possible to the original tempo and style. It doesn't have to be exactly the same, but the closer, the better. This time just shoot medium shots and close-ups. Also shoot 2-shots and big close-ups. Concentrate on action shots. You may have to ask the band to play a third time to get all the shots you need. The more variety you have the better. Each time record live sound as well. It will not be used as such when you edit, but it will be useful in cueing up inserts at the right place.

If it's not possible to get a decent sound recording of the number where you are shooting, use a copy of a demo soundtrack. The band mimes to that for the video recording of the master shot. Another possibility is to link via a sound mixer into the band's amplifier output. Both these methods mean, however, that you will lose atmos sound on the master shot.

If you insert edit into the master shot itself, you will have to be sure not to make any mistakes! Insert editing is a once and for all edit. Once you record an insert edit over the original master shot, the original is gone forever. Make a copy of the master shot, and use that to insert edit into. The quality won't be as high, because you are losing one generation. But any mistakes won't be irrevocable, because the master will still be intact.

If the picture quality of the master shot is particularly poor, then you may *have* to insert into it. If so, practise first on a copy, to get the timing of shots sorted out. Something to watch with all insert editing is that the quality of the master and the inserts is not vastly different. If it is, the visual continuity of the programme will be disturbed. This might be a problem where you are using inserts direct from a camcorder or camera, for example titles, graphics, pictures, and so on.

Don't try to make the inserts too short, unless you deliberately want to make the edits have a jerky effect. Use two TVs or monitors during editing to make sure that the inserts keep continuity with the master at the In and Out points. Music video offers the opportunity to use a variety of special effects. These should add to the overall effect, rather than distract. Try to work on a theme or motif for the video. Work with the artist or band to decide the atmosphere you want to create.

There is no reason why the artist or band has to be seen playing at all. You could shoot a short video film, drama, montage or animation. Once the soundtrack is on tape, you can insert whatever you like. Sometimes a visual effect might involve breaking the normal rules of visual continuity. Don't be afraid to experiment and to use your own ideas. Originality is a rare and much sought after commodity.

HOW TO USE VIDEO FOR SURVEY AND ANALYSIS

Video is an ideal medium to record the development of a project, and for systems analysis. Portable video can easily be taken to the production site or assembly line. It can be used to record each crucial stage of development, to show before and after scenes. These can be invaluable in assessing the progress of a project, and comparison with developments elsewhere.

Recordings can be made at fixed intervals over time. These can be stored and later shown to the client to demonstrate the rate of progress. In systems analysis, the same technique can be used to identify bottlenecks and problem areas. Record-only VCRs, with minimal facilities, are all that is required for this sort of application, which would help to make it cost-effective. In some circumstances, inexpensive black and white cameras could be quite adequate.

VCRs which have long play are ideal to show up faults in machinery which happen only periodically or intermittently. A camera can be left recording the machine in operation for up to eight hours at a time, depending upon format. Replay at fast search speed will soon identify when and where the problem occurs. It is doubly effective to use a built-in timer to pinpoint exactly when the faults occur, and over what sort of length of time they occur. A clock left in shot will, however, do just as well.

Video has applications for surveys in town and country planning, architecture and construction engineering. Any changes and transformations made over a set time span can be accurately recorded. For example, visual evidence could be shown to planners, of the effect of a short term experiment in providing free parking for supermarket customers in local authority car parks. Visual sequences showing the differences in on-street parking before and after the experiment, is a far more effective way of showing the reduction in congestion, than simply producing a batch of figures or a static graph.

HOW TO MAKE A VIDEO ARCHIVE

A video archive is a fascinating way of gathering together historical and geographical information on a local area. This could be done purely out of interest in, and love of, an area, or as an educational project, or as a commercial venture. An audio-visual record is a sure way to bring a place, or a by-gone age, to life.

Your first job will be to research your subject. Fortunately, local records are usually freely available and well-kept and preserved. Fruitful sources of information and records might be the public library, museum, local history and geography society, and churches. These should provide you with most of your documented sources.

Next, research guide books of the area, and history or geography books, to brief yourself on the most likely locations. Then, armed with a notepad, and possibly a stills or video camera ('snapshots' only at this stage, though), set off to visit your potential locations.

By now you should have a feel for how you might approach the programme. The next stage is to track down people who would be able and willing to be interviewed. Ideally, you want people who have interesting stories to tell, and who tell them in an equally interesting way. It is best to shoot these interviews early on in the production, as you will need to use them in deciding what cutaways you will need. Many of the visual sequences of the programme may well be based on these interviews. A lot depends on how fruitful the interviews are.

Before interviewing your subjects, prepare some good questions. Avoid ones which can be answered by a straightforward 'yes' or 'no'. Your questions should start mostly with the letter 'W' – who, what, when, where, why . . . and how? Generally you will find that people are very forthcoming. Television still holds a fascination for most people. Usually, video cameras only make people shy in formal settings. If you set up the shot you want and leave it running while you conduct the interview, your subject will soon forget all about the camera.

If you are doing a voice-over commentary, note down any ideas for content as you are doing your research and visiting locations. You will have more vivid ideas that way, rather than sitting at a desk looking at a blank sheet of paper! You may find it helpful to take a sound tape recorder with you when you visit people and locations, so that any ideas for commentary can be instantly recorded when they occur.

You may like to try a 'then and now' sequence. Get hold of an old photograph of the area you are interested in. Take it with you to where it was taken, and set up as near as you can to where the photo was taken from. Shoot the photo, using macro, and de-focus. Take away the photo and re-focus, this time on the actual scene. This is an effective way of showing how the area has changed over the years. You may have to use pause between the two shots to get a smoother transition between them.

The idea of an archive is that it can be used as primary source material by the historians of the future. This does not mean that your video has to contain a lot of facts and figures. That can be done equally well, probably better, on paper. What video can contribute to those who want to know about a place or a time, is how people see things, what people speak like, what they speak about, what they wear. It is because video can mirror life so closely that it can provide its own unique contribution as an archive. As a programme maker, your job is to weave the limitless possibilities of subject and content into a coherent, enjoyable and interesting programme.

WHAT ELSE VIDEO IS USED FOR

Video is used in hundreds of different ways. Three of the more original are:

Video art   There is a strong video art movement in the UK and Europe. It is impossible to summarise it, because its origins and expression are diverse. Some video art uses traditional production values, obeying the unities of time and place. Sometimes it is the subject itself which marks out a video as art. There are quite bizarre videos which use deliberately off-set colour balance, confusing shots and angles. Others deliberately disobey visual continuity, to make the viewer conscious of the video recording process. Many art forms challenge our perception of the world. This can be done with video art simply by breaking the usual visual conventions.

Animation   Limited animation is possible with video. By using Record and Pause, still pictures can be moved slightly between each recording, so that on playback they appear to move. It is not possible to edit accurately enough on small-format video to get smooth, filmic-type animation, but the effect can be interesting and unusual. It is still necessary to originate on film and then do a tele-cine transfer if you want a conventional animated sequence in your video.

Scratch video   It is not necessary to have a video camera to make a scratch video. It uses pirate extracts from broadcast television, editing them in a new way to bring out a certain point or message. What is produced is a kind of video collage. Original material such as captions or live sequences shot with video can also be introduced to achieve more direct control over the mixture of images.

MAKING VIDEO AS A GROUP

Making a video programme on your own is quite possible, but often more can be done when there are one, two or several others to help. A video programme needs creativity and imagination. With a group, ideas can be talked around, and discussed. There are a lot of different aspects to a video production – direction, camera, VT (videotape) operator, sound, lighting, captions, continuity, editing. Some programmes may require a presenter, interviewer, or voice-over commentary. Programmes vary in the weight attached to each of these roles, but every programme features some of them. Trying to play all those roles, and to acquire all those skills is asking a lot of anyone, however talented. However, it is possible to overlap some roles. For example, when using a separate camera and VCR, the VT operator may also monitor the sound recording.

Making video with a group can be most enjoyable. There can be genuine delight when the various elements come together to make the final programme. But this will only happen if the group is organised. The traditional way of doing this is to assign exact jobs and responsibilities – production roles – to people. Each role has its own place in the whole production. The different roles need to be co-ordinated, and this is the job of the director.

The director must keep track of the overall aim and direction of the programme, and interpretation of the script. He or she is also responsible for co-ordinating all the other roles. The director is the one who will liaise between those who are going to be in front of camera, and those who will be behind. Sometimes the director is also the producer. The two terms are often used interchangeably, but if there is a difference, production has more to do with commission and administration, whilst the director has control over the artistic content of the programme. Directing is an art. As director, you will have to be able to organise people to do their jobs as best they can, and to handle people who might be appearing in front of camera for the first time.

The camera operator is probably the role that people are most familiar with. It may involve lighting as well, since the two are naturally interdependent, and many productions do not involve enough people to have a separate lighting specialist.

The camcorder operator would also start the VT running. The VT operator starts and stops the VCR, on cue from the director. Once everyone is ready, the director says 'run VT'. The VT operator runs VT, checks that the spools are turning, and that recording is taking place, and replies 'VT running'. This ritual is, in fact, very useful. It makes sure that the tape is started at the right time, every time. It lets everyone know that a take is about to be recorded. And when editing, it is a cue for continuity to hold the ident board in shot, and to start counting down from 10.

Members of the group will also have to look after locations, props, equipment, and general management of the technical side of the production. It is worth deciding beforehand who will take on these various jobs. Someone will have to cue the presenter, actor or actress, interviewer, or anyone who needs cueing. Mostly, of course, cues have to be done silently, or else they would be heard on tape. So visual cues are used. A visual cue should be a distinct arm movement.

The cue must always be given from the correct eyeline. If a presenter is speaking to camera, then the cue should be given from just below the lens. If an actress is supposed to be looking right of frame for a shot, then she must be cued from that direction. If the floor manager is standing out of her eyeline and therefore can't give the cue, then a cue can be given to someone else to give to the performer ('throwing' a cue).

In small crews, when the camera is separate from the VCR the sound operator is also the VT operator. The sound operator will generally hold or set up the microphone(s), and monitor sound levels during recording. It is not unusual for the sound operator to carry the VCR on the shoulder, wear headphones ('cans') plugged into the VCR, and hold a boom microphone below the frame, just out of shot. Two pairs of hands is a useful asset for looking after sound!

Scripting and captions can be combined with other roles, as they are done pre-production – although it has been known for productions to start before the script is finished! As editing takes place post-production, that can also be taken on by someone who has another crew position.

The continuity person is responsible for checking visual continuity from shot to shot. When programmes are edited, successive shots in the programme may be recorded days apart, so it is vital to keep tabs on what people wear, which way they are looking at the end of the shot, shot sizes, and so on. Also involved is the preparation of up-to-date scripts and booking facilities. Usually it is a catch-all job for anything the director forgets or can't be bothered to do, involving hard work and little glory!

Presentation, or being seen and heard, involves very different skills to those of production. The presenter, whether on screen or voice-over, is the direct link with the viewer. As such, the viewer will have certain expectations of what presenters say and do. These conventions were developed in broadcast television. They have a logical basis, and should be followed whenever you include an interview, presentation to camera, or voice-over in your programme.

HOW TO CONDUCT AN INTERVIEW, AND 'VOX POPS'

Interviews are a useful way of getting people to talk. The chances are that the person you interview will be nervous or apprehensive. You must show gentle control. To get the most out of the interviewee (respondent) it is important that you are well-prepared. You need to brief yourself thoroughly on the subject of the interview. If you don't, the respondent may well dry up, and you will be left with awkward pauses.

The interview technique itself is the same whether you are going to use the interview as it is, or as commentary with different pictures. Don't start straight in with the topic of the interview. Make the subject feel at ease first. Talk about the general areas you want to cover in the interview, but don't reveal the exact questions. If you do, the respondent will probably rehearse the answers, and they will be stale and unconvincing. Rehearsed interviews look and sound phony.

Decide the exact wording of your first question. That will help you get a good start to the interview. Then make brief notes for the other questions. If you over-prepare all the questions, it's more difficult to build on the answers you have already had. Listen to what the respondent says. Follow up interesting points and leads, and don't be afraid to depart from your notes.

Ask short concise questions, avoiding ones that can be answered by a simple 'yes' or 'no'. If the respondent gets stuck on a question, go on. It is better to come back to a topic, rather than try to force an answer that just isn't there. You will save a lot of editing time if you can ask the questions in the order you are likely to want the answers. This may seem obvious, but it is surprising how often interviews end up being completely re-edited to fit the programme structure.

Encourage the respondent to use simple everyday language. Point out that video is one to one. It is personal and intimate. Statements and high-sounding words are out of place. Remember this yourself if you do a link or summary direct to camera.

Interview snippets are often used to present a range of popular opinion. They are called 'vox pops' (from the Latin *vox populi*, meaning the voice of the people). Vox pops are simply a collection of interview answers, edited together to make a continuous sequence.

Vary the background, shot size and angle when you shoot vox pops, so that there will be some visual variety when they are edited. Avoid interrupting the respondent. If you say 'yes', or 'mmm', or anything else, you will make editing all the more difficult. Remember, for the same reason, to wait for two or three seconds at the end of an answer, before you ask the next question or thank the respondent.

When editing vox pops, you can either edit the first question and answer, followed by further answers, or introduce the sequence to camera, saying something like: 'Feelings are running high over the proposed cutbacks', followed by the first vox pop.

When you are doing a direct-to-camera link to a location recording, the accepted way is to look away from camera when you finish the link, as though looking at a TV or monitor, and waiting for the location sequence to start. The link will appear quite natural if you do this.

HOW TO STAY ON THE RIGHT SIDE OF THE LAW

Copyright music Musical works are in copyright up to 50 years after the composer's death. After that time, the work is out of copyright, and no permission is necessary to use it, nor royalties payable.

However, an old song or hymn may have more recent lyrics. If this is so, then the whole work is protected by copyright.

If you make a video which has live performance of copyright music being played on it, you must pay a fee for a licence from the Mechanical Copyright Protection Society (MCPS). Their address is: The Video Department, MCPS, Elgar House, 41 Streatham High Road, London SW16 1ER. They welcome telephone enquries on 01–769 4400.

For weddings, dances, parties and other private functions where there is live music, there are two kinds of licence available:

1. for individuals (wishing to record one occasion only);

2. for companies or persons intending to video record a number of functions.

MCPS is a society of composers and publishers. The licences cover video recording of live performance of all MCPS members' musical works. MCPS do not need to know the individual pieces of music concerned, and you may apply for the licence before the music has been chosen.

The individual licence costs £5.75 and permits you to make up to 10 videos, i.e. 1 master and 9 copies. These must not be sold or exploited commercially in any way.

The company licence covers up to 15 productions in 12 months for £57.50. Additional productions cost £3.83 each. You do not need to be a company to apply for this licence.

There is a third licence which covers use of Mood Music Library works used in post-production. Library Mood Music is specifically written to be used in videos and other media. The licence permits unlimited recording of mood music for any one production. It costs £34.50, permitting 10 copies to be made. To apply for one of these licences, ask for a music cue sheet from MCPS. Once it is completed and returned to MCPS, you will be sent an invoice. Allow at least two weeks before the required date when applying for licences.

There is also a separate copyright in *recorded* sound on disc and tape and thus need a separate licence to re-record the tape or disc onto video, as well as any licence(s) required from MCPS.

For further information on sound recordings, contact Phono-graphic Performance Limited, Ganton House, 14 Ganton Street, London W1. Tel: 01–437 0311.

There is an organisation, set up over 50 years ago, called the Institute of Amateur Cinematographers. They exist to promote the interests of *amateur* film makers and, latterly, video makers and have nogotiated reduced rates for the clearance of copyright in certain circumstances. Membership of the Institute is currently £8.00 a year for members of a film or video society affiliated to IAC, and £12.50 for others. Age concessions apply to those under 21 and over 65. Full details can be obtained from the Administrative Secretary, Institute of Amateur Cinematographers Ltd, 63 Woodfield Lane, Ashtead, Surrey KT21 2BT.

The fees quoted above were correct at the time of writing but may, of course, be subject to variation.

Photographs   Photographs are subject to copyright. If you want to use a photograph as part of your programme, for example as a caption, you must seek the permission of the photographer. If you don't know who the photographer was, then you are expected to make all reasonable efforts to trace him or her. You may simply be asked to give a programme credit, or pay a fee, or both. Note that any fee paid is for a specific use of a photograph; ownership remains with the photographer.

The best single source of photographs is a photographic agency. An agency will have a number of photographers on their books, and will handle distribution, fees and royalty payments. A list of the main agents, their addresses and specialisations can be found in *Writers' and Artists' Yearbook* (published annually by Adam & Charles Black).

Off-air recording   All off-air recording, sound and video, breaks copyright. Most broadcast programmes are 'cinematograph films' within the meaning of the 1956 Copyright Act, and thus copies can only be made by the copyright holder, not the private viewer.

In addition, the rights of others who have contributed to the programme are infringed by copying – music composers, for example, and authors of books on which a television programme may be based.

Educational users can record certain educational programmes, but only with prior agreement by the relevant broadcasting company.

Making copies of off-air programmes and selling or hiring them, is fraud. So is making copies of commercial videos ('videograms'), regardless of whether they are for private or public viewing.

The Act also extends to cable television, films and sound broadcasts. Successful prosecutions under the Act have established that ignorance, no matter how reasonable, is no defence.

Shooting in the street   You are entitled to record what you like in a public place: in the street, for example. You may record people, buildings, or any scene in actual life. No-one can sustain a legal objection to being recorded in public. However, to avoid misunderstanding, you should ask anyone who is featured in an interview to sign a release, simply stating that he or she agrees to you using the interview in any programme you are making.

You are, of course, like everyone else, subject to the law of the land. Making a video recording will not, in itself, put you in breach of the law. But it may do so indirectly. For example you can be sued if someone trips over a cable and is injured, or is burnt by a carelessly placed lamp.

If you are shooting in a busy street, with equipment and leads sprawled all over the pavement, you could reasonably expect to be warned of causing an obstruction. Similarly, if you are making a programme in a public place, it will often attract a crowd of people. As the person responsible for attracting the throng, you could be charged with causing an obstruction.

If your production is at all likely to attract attention or cause obstruction, make a prior call to the local police station. They will appreciate the consideration, and will be able to advise you on what you may and may not do. And do be aware that if you shoot anywhere near a defence installation or 'prohibited place' you may infringe the Official Secrets Act which can be a very serious offence.

Overseas law   Some overseas governments are very sensitive about photographs being taken near official buildings, factories, airports, military installations, etc. Soldiers and policemen are often camera-shy. Video will be regarded with equal, if not more, suspicion. Use common sense at all times, and especially when using video away from normal tourist areas.

It is sometimes required by the customs authorities of other countries, and always advisable in any case, to carry a list of all equipment and tapes you take overseas. You may be asked to leave a copy with customs when you enter the country. This may be produced by the authorities when you leave the country, and, if there are any missing items, you will be asked to account for them. If you cannot, (and it is often difficult to do so), it will be assumed that you have sold them. Expect to pay tax on the estimated sale price.

Some countries require you to complete a carnet, to deposit with customs, which avoids any misunderstandings about what you are taking in and taking out. If you should lose your equipment, or have it stolen, make sure that you report the loss to the police for insurance purposes, and also get a letter from them to use at customs. Arrive early if there is any possible irregularity that needs to be sorted out.

AFTERWORD

If you choose video as a medium to use as a hobby, at work, as a business, to take on holiday, I hope that you will want to improve your knowledge and your technique. Reading books and magazines is a first step. Courses might help, depending on their level and quality, and how much practical experience they offer.

Whether you use video for pleasure, or gain, or perhaps both, you can learn most from your own efforts with a camcorder or camera. Try out techniques and ideas for yourself. Use this book as a source of advice, but apply it to your own videos. If you are frequently disappointed, examine your work critically. Learn from your mistakes *and* your successes.

Try not to be too ambitious at first. Keep to procedures and techniques that you know. Introduce new ideas one at a time, so that you can judge properly whether they work. If in doubt, adopt the simplest approach. It's usually the best.

SELECTED BOOK AND MAGAZINE LIST

Books

Professional video international yearbook ed. by S. Baker. Link House Magazines Ltd, annual.
A comprehensive guide to professional video equipment, including lighting and other accessories (but not audio), plus lots of other useful information, such as manufacturers' and dealers' addresses and telephone numbers.

ELLIOTT, G. *Video production techniques* Kluwer Publishing, 1980.
A comprehensive practical handbook on video, film and tape-slide production. The format is looseleaf, with regular updates sent to subscribers every four months.

GASKILL, A. AND ENGLANDER, D. *How to shoot a movie and video story: the technique of pictorial continuity* New York: Morgan and Morgan, 1985.
Available in UK from Henry Greenwood & Co., 28 Great James Street, London WC1N 3HL. The basic text is 40 years old, but it has been recently revised and remains an excellent primer on visual continuity.

MILLERSON, G. *Video camera techniques* Focal Press, pbk, 1983.
Covers the operation and use of a video camera, with useful hints on common problems.

WATTS, H. *On camera: how to produce film and video* BBC Publications, rev. edn pbk, 1984.

Magazines

Audio Visual published by Maclaren, PO Box 109, Maclaren House, Scarbrook Road, Croydon CR9 1OH. Available monthly by limited circulation to those working in video in commerce, industry, education, etc., or direct from the publisher. Covers all AV media, with occasional helpful features on production techniques.

Making Better Movies published by Henry Greenwood & Co., 28 Great James St, London WC1N 3HL. Available monthly from larger newsagents and bookstalls. There's a distinct film-based pedigree (the magazine incorporates *Amateur Cine World* (established 1934), *Movie Maker, Cine Camera* and *Film Making*). Not surprisingly, it's weighted to 8mm cine-film enthusiasts, but worth getting, as much applies equally to video. Also good equipment reviews and special video features.

Televisual published by Centaur Communications Ltd, St Giles House, 49/50 Poland St, London W1V 4AX. Available monthly by limited circulation or direct from the publisher. For independent producers, facilities houses and the broadcast industry. Wide and authoritative coverage, mostly concentrates on the top end of the AV marketplace.

What Video published by WV Publications Ltd, Third Floor, City House, London EC1N 7TR. Available monthly from newsagents and bookstalls. Features, reviews and news on small-format video, with a regular section on creative video, plus equipment prices and advice.

Index